HOUSETOPS—PRAGUE
Dr. D. J. Ruzicka

Principles of
Pictorial Photography

By JOHN WALLACE GILLIES

Used as a Supplementary Text in

NEW YORK INSTITUTE OF PHOTOGRAPHY

NEW YORK   CHICAGO   BROOKLYN

———

Published and Copyrighted by

Falk Publishing Company, Inc.
145 West 36th Street, New York

Individual Conceptions of Pictorial Photography

By

CLARENCE H. WHITE   EDWARD WESTON
DR. A. D. CHAFFEE   ALEXANDER P. MILNE
O. C. REITER   W. H. PORTERFIELD
NICKOLAS MURAY

An Unexcelled Display of Exceptional Prints Produced by the Following Celebrated Pictorialists

DR. A. D. CHAFFEE   LAURA GILPIN
DR. D. J. RUZICKA   CHARLES K. ARCHER
CLARA E. SIPPRELL   O. C. REITER
THOMAS O. SHECKELL   ALICE BROUGHTON
CHARLES ALBIN   FRANCIS BRUGUIERE
NICKOLAS MURAY   ALEXANDER P. MILNE
W. H. PORTERFIELD   PAUL OUTERBRIDGE, JR.
EDWARD WESTON   ADELE C. SHREVE
EDITH WILSON   JOSEPH R. MASON
MARGARET DeM. BROWN   MERCEDES DESMORE

CONTENTS

LIST OF ILLUSTRATIONS

AN APPRECIATION

IN attempting this book I have chosen to present the opinions of others besides myself, on the ground that no one opinion meant anything; that the whole matter of pictures in any form was merely what one or the other thought about the thing, and if any opinion could be ventured at all it must necessarily be taken from the consensus of the opinions of those who knew it best. In the years that I have lived with photography it has been my good fortune to become associated with many fine characters who represented the backbone of the work, and when it came time to say something about it, these were the persons to whom it was natural to turn in the emergency.

From long years ago, Mr. White has been my good friend and adviser, and while I hold myself at perfect liberty to disagree with anything he says, it has been a most amicable difference at all times. and indeed a pleasant one. One would almost rather have Clarence White to disagree with, than most persons to be chummy with. It has indeed been a pleasant and profitable friendship, for me. To him I turn therefore for much of my advice upon photography, and it's whys.

From Dr. Chaffee I have had many of the finer thoughts which I have carried with me over the years, and while he has a very humorous viewpoint upon photography and photographers, and takes them none too seriously, he has assumed one of the rather terrible burdens for himself as the chief executive of the Pictorial Photographers. His only pleasure in photography must therefore be, when he can take refuge in his immaculate bromoil prints, and forget organizations.

In Mr. Porterfield I feel that I have a real friendship, and while he and I have never met each other, we have bombarded each other with many reams of paper, all covered with writing, and much has been said. He is one of the inspirational workers in photography, and is for its good.

As I write this immature dissertation upon photography, I hear the message of my fine friend, Weston, calling across three thousand miles of continent, that I should take it seriously, when he knows very well that it is too impossible. He is one of the rare characters in photography, and I need not add one of its greatest workers.

I turn to Reiter for his knowledge of all photographic workers, and he responds by saying something for my book. Who could do it as well as he, with his intimate knowledge of all in Pictorial Photography? He has been the master organizer of pictorialists.

When my thoughts turn to technique, I have but to lift the telephone and at my disposal are the opinions of men like Muray and Milne, perhaps the two greatest technicians in photography. The former has built a sound technique upon ten years' experience in photo-engraving, where immaculate work is required, and it has shown itself in his pictorial work. Milne has enlightened me on many points of photographic chemistry and knows it better than any person I have met, and when I desire to find a man who really understands what a soft focus lens can do, I can do no better than to ask him. He knows.

For my information upon the history of photography there was but one unprejudiced man I could turn to, John Tennant. He has looked sometimes with amusement, sometimes with concern, upon the little drama of photography for thirty years and sees it with the unbiased eye of the spectator.

To these men I owe much, and when I need knowledge of any kind, technical or compositional, I can find anything I want from one of them. They know. It has indeed been a great experience to explore the minds of these men whom I call friends, when I needed information, and to see more of them in this manner than I ever knew before. They are a foundation upon which any worker in photography can well build a solid ground from which to start.

If there are any in all photography who know it better than these, in their several branches, the writer has not found them. It has been an inspiration to be near them.

JOHN WALLACE GILLIES

STILL LIFE
Adele C. Shreve

JAPANESE FENCING MASK
Edward Weston

INTRODUCTION

IN most cases where books are written the writer carefully writes his book and after that writes the introduction. In this case we propose to write the introduction first, which is quite wrong. Nobody ever knows what he is going to say before he says it, no matter how well he knows his subject. No more do we, and yet do we propose to tell of what we are going to do before we do it.

We are not going to be too serious in this book. It will be better reading. While the subject is more or less important, we will not be too heavy with it. Nothing is serious in this poor world, except perhaps, to meddle with ideas knowingly, and we do not do that. Many will say that we touch not upon ideas at all. And yet we do, under the guise of lighter words. Let him read deeper, into our lightness.

Pictorial Photography is a pleasant thing. It is a great boon to the man who cannot draw, and yet would create pictures. In fact, most of us who live in it are persons who late in life find out that we have an impulse toward picture creation, and have not the skill to set it down in paint or other medium. We find it out through photography, not having realized the charm of pictures before taking up the camera. At first we took it up as a hobby, and made records, as all do, except the few. Then we

15

saw that with the camera we could make pictures. Hence the pictorial photograph. This is the history of about ninety percent of pictorial workers.

In this book, we are not going to be too technical, It makes dry reading, and that is criminal. The world is full of dry discourse that nobody will read. While it is perfectly good material, well written, academic, and knowing, it is dry. So nobody will read it except those few good souls who read everything, mostly dry. We are going to see if the idea of pictorial photography cannot be told practically and simply to the man who does not know, so that he will understand it.

It is no use for us to try to educate Dr. Ruzicka or Edward Weston. They do not need our teaching. They know what they know, and are all settled in their ways, and need no help. The worker who is coming is the man who needs the help we can give, and the pictures of tomorrow depend to some extent upon what help we of today can extend.

So we propose to tell the new worker about Pictorial Photography in the simplest of terms and, above all, we hope to be practical. It is a terrible thing to "hitch" the word practical to Pictorial Photography, and yet we do it, perhaps for the first time in history. We stand upon that point, and refuse to budge. It is about time something practical was done about Pictorial Photography. We have seen the "arty" ones parading about, with long words and waving hands, talking balance, unity and other things, when they could not make a proper negative,

"POPLARS"
W. H. Porterfield

RENAISSANCE
Dr. A. D. Chaffee

and the writer believes that the negative has a lot to do with the picture. The world is full of good chaps who do not know the chemical constituents of their developers, and we believe that this is one of the things a good photographer should know. As it happens, most good artists know the chemistry of their colors, and while we do not choose to compare photography with paint, we at least can draw the comparison that the good photographer of a necessity must know what occurs in his medium. He must know the character of his emulsions, why they do this, and why they do that, in order that he can proceed with surety. He must base his progress upon a sound technique or he is lost.

Inspiration and technique are so mixed up with each other that we cannot separate them. In the first place the "artist" has an inspiration. For a long time that is all he has except failure. Then he begins to develop a technique, and to see that he can do certain things. He gets new ideas, and when he has taken one step successfully he sees that he can build another upon it. He has new inspiration to go ahead. Technique is builded, and upon it inspiration is placed, one upon the other until he has a structure of both entwined together.

So the embryo pictorial worker is urged to build up his technique, but never to forget that all he does it for is to make pictures. He must not become lost in a maze of formulae and figures. There are those in photography who would rather read a lens catalog than make a print. They have strayed into

19

technical matters. In fact, they may never have had the pictorial impulse at all. The thought throughout is to hold to the idea of "the picture." Everything you do, is but to assist in making a better picture and, if the course is held, one will succeed by sheer doggedness.

CHAPTER I.

STATEMENTS

BY

CLARENCE H. WHITE   O. C. REITER
DR. A. D. CHAFFEE   ALEXANDER P. MILNE
EDWARD WESTON   W. H. PORTERFIELD
NICKOLAS MURAY

IN the Pictorial section of photography one can make almost any kind of statement he pleasese, and some will nod sagely, "Yes" and others will disagree with great heat. It is right or wrong as it happens to strike the other fellow. There is nothing absolute, nothing settled. It is an art, or not an art as we please to have it. Stieglitz at present makes his pictures sharp and is ready to tell everybody that a fuzzy picture is not the thing. Clarence White likes his pictures softer, and has held to that view, which speaks well for his first opinion. Steichen made them fuzzy years ago, and now cannot get them sharp enough. So what are we to think? Each one has something to say and each statement is different. One might think from this that Pictorial Photography must be an art, for we find the same conditions among painters, all wrangling about what is best. True it is, therefore, that photographers have all the indispositions of artists and, if that makes art, we surely have it in photography.

The writer is at a loss as to what to say about it, although he does not fear dispute because nobody else knows anything about it. While it is not an easy task, he believes that a picture can be made by photography and that there are many doing it. But there are certain elements which militate against it and there is a grave question if the photographic picture will ever stand the test, so that it will endure as a permanent work of art. Whether photography is an art or not, is not the case. We do not care about that. It is an unfortunate question and has been applied too many times. It is as sensible to say, "Is a woodcarver's process a work of art?" Nothing is a work of art that is not really a creation of the brain and impulses of man, but any such thing really is. No process can be called a work of art.

In photography certain things are so mechanical that there is grave question whether there is enough of the element of craftmanship involved, whether the photograph is not too much the victim of lenses and chemicals, and whether it allows enough of the creative sense of the man to operate. When the lens is adjusted to make the picture, is its work not too mechanical? When the chemicals are used, are they not too uncontrollable? Only the question of control of craftsmanship exists in the writer's mind, the picture part being beyond dispute. One can arrange as well in photography as in any other process. One can control many things. But the full control of values, as to delineation of proper line and mass, is in question. Has the photographer the choice of textures as the painter has? Unquestionably the hand

22

STUDY IN BALANCE
Paul Outerbridge, Jr.

"WORK"
Joseph R. Mason

craft picture has many advantages over the machine-made picture, and still we are not sure about this art matter.

Under these circumstances we turn to certain persons who are well-known in photography as real picture makers, and whose opinions ought to have a value. They will perhaps tell us something about it and their statements are printed herewith.—EDITOR.

By Clarence H. White

Dear Mr. Gillies:

I took up photography, as nine out of ten of the photographers do, as a hobby, and pursued it with all the enthusiasm of the amateur—so much so that a change of occupation became necessary. Photography then became my real work, but I was still anxious to keep the attitude of the amateur by doing the best in me. I believed in photography as an *expression for an artist*. This persistence led me into another field of photography, that of teaching.

After thirty years of experience, I feel that I can accomplish now what I thought at the first could be done in a year or so. I still have a thrill when I think I am on the right road, and a little envy when I see a beginner who appears to have arrived.

CLARENCE H. WHITE

PHOTOGRAPHY
Dr. A. D. Chaffee

Many roads lead toward Rome, though not all of them extend so far; and of those that do reach there, and even of those that begin at the same point, no two remain identical or terminate in the same quarter of that desirable city. For each road has been beaten by some traveller for himself, and becomes thereafter his path, not to be shared with nor followed by another.

Which means, in part, that most of us derive our initial enthusiasm in pictorial photography from the work of others and the desire to make pictures such as we have seen. But, so long as we consciously or unconsciously imitate—so long as we go out to do "something like that," or so long as we go out *and* do "something like that"—we are following somebody's else road, which for us will be no road toward anything but a mirage.

We must begin, of course, with the objects in front of our cameras that others have used; we must employ their tools and processes. No magic resides in camera or type of lens or printing method; a bromoil is not better than a bromide, or vice versa. No instrument but the seeing eye makes the picture; no paper or process renders it except in the hands of one who can put individuality into his technique. Do not think you have mastered photography because you have made a wire sharp image of an object with an anastigmat, or because, on the other hand, you have achieved a fuzzy one with an uncorrected lens; nor because you have made a muddy bromide or evolved a granular gum, or got a smudgy image and inky fingers out of bromoil.

It is proper to study what others have done in

photography and other pictorial media and to listen to criticism, in order to get an impetus toward doing something of your own, and often, to learn what to avoid. Good equipment usually makes for convenience and for some subjects and conditions it is a necessity; but choose your lens, finally, because you have learned to use it for yourself and like what you can do with it. Study processes and their results in the hands of experts to learn their possibilities—not to make prints like So-and-So's—but to mould the method to your own needs and tastes. Of so-called control processes and straight photography, neither can be said to be better than the other, much less can either be considered exclusively the right thing. As a matter of fact, all processes submit themselves to more or less control when used by workers skilled in them. Control in any process must be intelligent to a degree; if so, I believe it not only justifiable but advantageous; if unskillful, it is probably a crime, though as yet unrecognized by the courts.

When at the last you shall have recorded your own vision in your own way, you may be considered to have won through to your own lodgings in the Imperial City, perhaps only in its outskirts or slums, but with the prospect before you of moving into better and better neighborhoods. And your way has become your own way, and you also cannot share it. You cannot teach your vision and your method to another or, if you can, they still remain your own and not that of others, and are worthless to him.

And do not commit the final error of assuming

that your way and your results are the only methods and the only desirable end. The other fellow is probably doing just as good work as yourself and, however different it may be, quite as right and true. It may, indeed, be far better.

In fact, the permanent value of your work is not of supreme importance; for while the opinion of thoughtful contemporaries is something of a guide, only time and posterity can render the final verdict, and you cannot wait for the one nor hear of the other. But the work will have been valuable to yourself insofar as it has been a sincere following of a personal idea; the question of its intrinsic worth can well be pigeonholed, along with those classic futilities, "Is Photography Art?" and "What is Art?"

———

By Edward Weston

Dear Gillies:—

You ask me to write a short *ms.* on "Pictorial Photography," in other words, "illustrative photography," for such is my understanding of the word pictorial. Well I cannot, for it has been years since I left the genre field, and anyhow there are so many painters well fitted to carry on this little by-product of literature. Forgive me, Gillies, for playing with words, but really, is not just "Photography" good or bad, significant without "Pictorial" or "Artistic" tacked on?

Again, you ask for "its reasons, hopes, requirements, ends, and what a man should be and try for, to be successful." Immediately my thoughts turn back to a series of intensely interesting and understanding articles on photography, written around Stieglitz and what he symbolizes, all published within the last year or two. So if I quote from them, and bring together a prose "Waste Land" of photographic notes, it should be more valuable than my lone and hurriedly jotted thoughts.

Now then, for a few "reasons," and I quote John Tennant on the Stieglitz exhibit—"A demonstration of what Hurter and Driffield years ago asserted to be 'the most valuable distinction of photography, i. e., its capacity to truthfully represent natural objects, both as regards delineation and light and shade.' A revelation of the ultimate achievement of photography, controlled by the eye and hand of genius and utterly devoid of trick, device or subterfuge." And further, "in the Stieglitz prints you have the subject itself, in its own substance or personality, as revealed by the natural play of light and shade about it, without disguise or attempt at interpretation, simply set forth with perfect technique," and from Paul Rosenfeld in The Dial—"Never, indeed, has there been such another affirmation of the majesty of the moment. No doubt, such witness to the wonder of the here, the now, was what the impressionist painters were striving to bear, but their instrument was not sufficiently swift. For such immediate response, a machine of the nature of the camera was required." Good reason, indeed, for photography's existence.

Its "hopes," Paul Strand writes in *The Broom*—
"In thus disinterestedly experimenting, the photographer has joined the ranks of all true seekers after knowledge, be it intuitive and aesthetic or conceptual and scientific. He has moreover, in establishing his own spiritual control over a machine, the camera, revealed the destructive and wholly fictitious mass of antagonism which these two groups have built around themselves. Rejecting all Trinities and all Gods, he puts to his fellow workers this question squarely, 'What is the relation between science and expression?' Are they not both vital manifestations of energy whose reciprocal hostility turns the one into the destructive tool of materialism, the other into anaemic fantasy, whose coming together might integrate a new religious impulse? Must not these two forms of energy converge before a living future can be born of both?' "

What a forecast—what a hope.

Its "requirements"—from Sherwood Anderson in "The New Republic"—"It has something to do with the craftsman's love of his tools and his materials. In an age when practically all men have turned from that old male love of good work well done and have vainly hoped that beauty might be brought into the world wholesale, as Mr. Ford manufactures automobiles, there has always been here in America this one man who believed in no such nonsense, who perhaps often stood utterly alone, without fellows, fighting an old man's fight for man's old inheritance— the right to his tools—his materials, and the right

30

to make what is sound and sweet in himself articulate through his handling of tools and materials."

Its "ends"?—read Herbert J. Seligman in "The Nation"—"What is it that this despised box, fitted with lens and shutter and called the camera, has done in this man's hands? It has penetrated the fear which human beings have of themselves lest those selves be made known to others. So doing it has laid bare the raw material which life in America has not yet dared look upon and absorb. When Americans are ready to undertake inquiry about themselves, their nation, the world, as the camera has been made to inquire, there may dawn a sense of common humanity."

And finally "what should a man be and try for"— Paul Rosenfeld in "The Dial"—"Stieglitz"—"For himself, so his works attest, has always been willing to live every moment as though it were the last of his life, the last left him to expend his precious vitality. He himself has always been willing, in order to fix the instant, the object before him, and to record all that lay between him and it, to pour out his energy with gusto and abandon"—and further "And in ourselves, too, confronted by these noble monuments, there surges a great yea-saying to life, 'We too, before the works of this man who has included things great and small in his sympathy, who has accepted so freely his own moment, his own life, the pain as well as the beauty of the world; we, too, find the will to accept to the utmost the present, even though it be the present of a turmoiled world, a raw

31

America, to see what there is directly in front of us, to express ourselves in terms of our own time, to live in our own careers'."

My dear Gillies, need I say more?

EDWARD WESTON.

Editor's Note.—Mr. Weston, my very good friend and a man of impeccable honesty, has fallen in with words, written by gentlemen who use them to hide behind. With the exception of Sherwood Anderson and John Tennant, these gentlemen who talk glibly about the logic of things, using photography as a blind, are all more or less lost in delusion, and smoke a sort of mental pipe together when they produce their manuscripts.

We find America under the criticism of two gentlemen, named Seligman and Rosenfeld. Need America do anything except proceed upon its way without reply?

Happily there is no doubt about Alfred Stieglitz, his being perhaps the finest thought in photography.

PICTORIAL PHOTOGRAPHY.—WHY?

O. C. Reiter

It is one of the most fascinating and useful of the arts, if the student applies himself, and it soon becomes second nature. It is a normal human impulse to desire to reproduce some thought or theme, strength of character, some beautiful subject, the sturdy artisan at his task in the grime and smoke of

STILL LIFE
Ira W. Martin

"THE SMOKY CITY"
Charles K. Archer

his labor. It is but healthy and normal to desire to picture the beautiful lines of the human form, to place in correct values the landscape in its different moods.

To be versatile in any art takes a lifetime. To every one is not given the power to portray varied subjects. To concentrate on a few and do them well, is best. Learn to use the tools properly, study carefully the work of masters. If we do this we acquire a style or thought of our own, and individual expression follows.

What satisfies most in what we do, is something that truly pleases, and of which we do not tire. A picture that stirs the pathos of one's being—which brings up in us some emotion, some thought, is one which will hold its position upon the wall. Or if you please to do so, a picture which reproduces the massive feeling of some great structure, in lights and shades. All of these may be gained by careful and hard work, but the greatest satisfaction comes at last when beautiful things have been produced.

Is Pictorial Photography worth while? Visit the collections that are gathered together in our best exhibitions, and the answer will be apparent. The scope of Pictorial Photography is far reaching, and it is forging ahead with great speed. It brings out the finer senses and incites emotions that lie dormant otherwise. The success of the student is determined by application, observation, selection and determination.

PHOTOGRAPHY AS A FINE ART

Alexander P. Milne

It has long been the purpose of photography to establish itself as a legitimate art, but there still remains in the minds of many of its critics the feeling that it has thus far failed to do so.

In considering the subject from as fair and unbiased a standpoint as possible, it must be admitted that this feeling is not without foundation in fact. Art must be essentially creative and not imitative, in the sense that any work of art of permanent value is the personal and individual expression of an idea. That fundamental idea whether new or old, expressed in the terms of individual conception and craftsmanship forms the basis and creation of all real art.

Photography to a large extent has not yet been placed upon this basis, however beautiful and artistic the way may be in which it has been presented. To be wholly frank it must be admitted that the bulk of photographs made have not been worked out from the individual conception of a basic idea, but rather the result of the seizure of an opportunity to record an interesting or beautiful subject. It is this feature more than all else that tends to keep photography in the ranks of mechanical processes.

The technical difficulties of the process, including its often too literal drawing and lack of plasticity, have turned many away from its serious consideration as an art medium. If then, photography is to

36

take a lawful place with other art, these difficulties and limitations must be overcome by the individual and the process used as a medium and not an end.

It is safe to say that photography will be generally recognized as an art when photographers or artists, working with the process as a medium only, produce pictures from a creative rather than a selective basis of such value as pictures alone that people will be attracted to them by the idea presented by the pictures rather than by the method by which they are made. _____

THE EDUCATIONAL VALUE OF PICTORIAL PHOTOGRAPHY

W. H. Porterfield

Some years ago a lively discussion centered around the question of photography as an art, painters and kindred craftsmen taking the negative, while advanced photographers attempted with considerable success to prove that it was. I say with considerable success, because it does not appear that the answer was properly expressed, and whatever the impression left by the debaters both sides still retained the opinions held at the beginning.

Whereas both were right, fundamentally, though both were wrong, in a measure, I should say that photography as practised by the majority of camera users has no claim to art. But pictures made by those who have studied and mastered the principles which are universally recognized as necessary, are art products and the persons are artists.

37

Aside from the result of the discussion the controversy had a far-reaching and beneficial effect, in that it brought to the attention of many people the possibilities of the camera. They became interested, lightly at first perhaps, but later discovered that the lens opened up to them visions of a new world and added to their knowledge of nature many phases little understood before.

Without fear of contradiction it can be said that everyone using a camera endeavors to make good photographs of whatever subject they may have chosen. They inquire regarding plates, paper and exposures, and all the elements which enter into the production of the picture. That in itself is educational. Their powers of observation are exercised and the ability to discriminate between different viewpoints is developed.

No one attempts to photograph an ugly thing. Time and effort are expended in searching for the beautiful, and all that is unlovely is passed by, or if it is given any consideration at all it is with the idea of effecting a transformation. Scenes and objects that under ordinary circumstances would be passed without notice are examined critically by the camerist, and beauty is found where it was not seen before.

Not the least of the benefits derived from association with the camera, is the fact that our views in time, undergo radical changes. We no longer look with contempt upon the common weed that blooms in an obscure fence corner, for there is beauty of

Dr. A. D. Chaffee

THE CITY
Dr. D. J. Ruzicka

design and great pictorial possibilities in such humble material. Many a masterpiece of photography had its inception in the lowly flora of a country wayside. One must, however, pause and draw near to the subject, study it carefully, not only with the eyes we have always known, but with the eye of the artist also. It is then that we begin to appreciate a little of the beauty which is everywhere about us. The weed may typify our first efforts in pictorialism, though we need not continue like the weed to dwell in obscurity and be satisfied with a place in a fence corner along life's road.

In time if we persist we shall leave behind us the barriers that once seemed insurmountable and understand that it was only our lack of knowledge that made them seem real. If photography does nothing more than teach us this one lesson it has served its purpose. Success is a comparative term and is obtainable by all who are willing to give the necessary attention to three primary requirements—honest desire, persistence, and practise, and not the least of these is practise.

On the Portrait

By Nickolas Muray

In a discussion on pictorial photography there are two angles from which this subject may be considered. There is first, personal preference in the choice of photographic processes and second, expediency or the method of procedure best suited under

41

given conditions. It is a simple matter to condemn operating methods of other photographers when one is carried away with his own individual views. But considering that through pictorial photography one tends to convey his personal artistic expression by means of the camera, it is hardly just to take exception to the methods employed by one's fellow photographers.

However, from the point of view of expediency one feels justified in voicing his likes and dislikes if he affords a rational explanation for them. In this connection there are three basic points upon which most photographers disagree and which are worthy of discussion. They are: (1) the use of the sharp or soft focus lens; (2) the length of exposure; (3) the question of retouching negatives.

I believe in the use of the soft focus lens, quick exposure, and a sensible use of the retouching pencil. It would be futile to thrust one's views upon anyone arbitrarily, so I shall endeavor to explain my attitude in the light of reason culled from past experiences.

I favor the soft focus lens because personally I am well satisfied in obtaining a pleasing, general effect as opposed to representing a subject in all its minutest detail. I am not arguing against showing detail or, for example, the necessary lines in a face which denote character, but I am not concerned with the number or distinctness of the pores in a sitter's face. I want my impression of people as seen through my own eyes at a reasonable distance and not through a magnifying glass. Nor do I desire to see them through a haze. Therefore, I don't strive for fuzziness or dimness in a picture. The soft focus lens— yes, but used intelligently. A face clear and characterful and neither befogged or "hair-line" sharp is the effect I try to achieve. For expediency I prefer the soft focus lens for its depth of field. I want the ear of my sitter to be as well defined as the tip of his nose, the hand on his knee as clear as his shoulder.

I advocate the short-time exposure. My idea of a well equipped studio is one where I can get a great amount of light properly placed and controlled cutting my exposure down to a minimum.

It is contended that with a comparatively quick exposure the same results are not obtainable as with a longer exposure; as for example, the character in the face of a sitter will lose in value in the former case. Scan, if you please, some of the pictures of the days of the head-rest and clamps and note the character depicted on the faces. If tenseness and a set expression exemplify character then I admit I am at fault. With a short exposure a fleeting glance, a twinkle of the eye, or a momentary mood is caught and this tells us more of a sitter than ten or twenty seconds of concentrated staring and tense muscles. With a short exposure one doesn't assume a natural expression; one has it in spite of oneself. With the aid of a silent shutter which is quite essential to set the sitter at ease, a bulb hidden from the sitter's gaze, a short exposure, and the latter registers the most natural expression without being at all aware of it.

I am also in favor of the intelligent use of the retouching pencil. No matter how sincere we may be in our art we still have to be photographically true to the sitter. If, by any chance, our subject has a well-rounded face with red cheeks, an unretouched negative would show these spots of red as hollow. If our plates lie to us we are duty bound to our sitter to rectify the error. The sitter isn't at all interested in the fact that red photographs black, and a few strokes of the retouching pencil will transform the sunken cheeks to their natural roundness. Besides, the average lens is unfriendly and unnecessarily severe in reproducing the human face. Ordinary blemishes are accentuated to a point beyond truth. A freckled face will pass inspection when seen in life but on the negative it becomes unsightly and inexcusable. Nor is it necessary to remove all lines which lend expression to a face. In using the pencil the retoucher must use his brains as well, lest he lose all semblance of the original. Modifying a negative to my mind is therefore absolutely essential when the camera gives me an overtruthful and erroneous representation of the subject.

After all, the camera can be made a medium by which we may express ourselves artistically no less than the painter's brush, but only when we make it serve us. In other words, we must make it and all its processes subject to our control and personal wish, if we are to attain individuality. Otherwise it becomes nothing less than a mechanical instrument making photography conventional and inartistic.

A DECORATIVE PANEL
Thos. O. Sheckell

PORTRAIT
A. P. Milne

Editor's Note:—

In arguing for the quick exposure as a means of catching mood or character, Mr. Muray is disputed by many venerable gentlemen in photography who still persist that a daguerrotype is better than any modern photograph. There will always be those who move forward, while looking backward, until they stumble upon some small obstacle and sit down in a most undignified manner.

There is no argument against Mr. Muray in this position and he is unquestionably right when he stands for the short duration of exposure. Else all modern photography has been devised for nothing and that cannot be so.

CHAPTER II.

THE PICTURE

WE are trying to place ourselves into the shoes of a man who has never been taught the qualities of Pictorial Photography. It is not so queer that there should be somebody who knows little about it, even if he is quite fair at making photographs. Pictorial Photography has developed a cult, as it happens, those who know about it and have lived in it long enough so that they cannot understand that there might be another person who does not think the same about things. He who knows nothing about Pictorial Photography is queer, and in saying so, it is taken that anybody is queer who is different from the person applying the name. So we turn to the man who knows less, since he is far more interesting than one who knows all about it. He at least has a race to run, and the fun of doing it, whereas the old stager has done his bit and there is nothing left for him to do but die.

We hope this newcomer will get this book and read it. He will, perhaps, find out that the camera has certain capabilities in the direction of picture making which make it quite a fascinating thing. How are we to reach this person and get him to look into the possibilities of Pictorial Photography? He has not thought about it, and the most difficult thing to do is to make another man change his thoughts. Wars are fought over just that. His camera has been to him a machine which made representations of certain people and events which in after years he took a certain pleasure in looking at and perhaps in showing to friends. Pictorial Photography is not at present in his landscape, and there are millions like him in the country. In fact, the great ninety-nine percent are just that way, the pictorialists being in a sad minority. However, since Ibsen said, "The minority is always right," we will take it for granted that we are right and set about luring the outsiders into the book, to see if we cannot change their thoughts. Their habits will follow. The great work is to get new workers thinking along better pictorial lines, and that's why this book is written. It is of no use to write a book for Dr. Ruzicka or Clarence White. There is nothing to teach them except, perhaps, to make a weak suggestion here and there. They have their ideas all settled, their ways laid out, and make their pictures as they please. They have been doing it a long time, and are well qualified to teach most of us. The book does them no good, except perhaps to amuse them that somebody could be so different and absurd as to disagree with what they know is right. They can read it, but not to their great gain. The person we desire to reach is the one who does not know so much about Pictorial Photography.

We, in photography, use words which are designated as vernacular, and which mean nothing to the outsider. Suppose you ask the average man what a Pictorial Photograph is. He will not be able to tell you. Yet we, in photography, are using the expression as meaning a photograph which has a special compositional and aesthetic value not at all found in the ordinary photograph. A particular kind of photograph, so to speak. We misuse the words, picture, picturesque and pictorial in order to specify a meaning. But we may as well accept them and make the most of it, as it will be difficult to coin new words, Shakespeare-like, for this book. It is important, however, since we should be able to make our definitions clear with words which the new worker can understand.

We come to the term, "Pictorial Photograph," and try to define its meaning as a photograph which has a special "art" value, not found in other photographs, they being of a merely reproductive nature. The Pictorial Photograph then, is one which has a value similar to that which we might find in a good painting; one which will convey an impression of some sort, or make one feel that it is more of a picture than the ordinary photograph. It is a very difficult thing to define. Let us then create our own definition for it. Let us say that "a picture is a graphical representation of some thing or things, which not only shows them, but shows them in such a manner that they mean something more to the observer than the representation of the mere objects, and conveys to him some emotion or idea." The picture we propose to discuss must reach out and take hold of a person and create in him some feeling, so that he will say that it is a wonderful picture and that he would like to have it to frame. Then we have made the successful pictorial photograph. No person, from the lowest to the highest, is proof against pictures. They are things which all men can understand. When they cannot understand each other in words, pictures mean the same things to them, and are a speech which any man knows.

We are much concerned in trying to find out what prompts a man to desire to make a picture, why he does it and what it is done for. Perhaps it will help us to know why we desire to make pictures. It is something worth while thinking of at any rate. At the present moment if some person should ask us why we desire to make a picture, we could not give him a reply which would satisfy us. We do not know, except that we like them very much.

At some time in the history of the world, somebody began the idea of making pictures. We are told that we were once reptiles and had no hands, and that gradually as the ages rolled by we developed into land animals and evolved into the present day man. From that it is apparent that pictures did not always exist, and that at one time in history some man, or some animal began making them for the first time. We can assume many things, and for lack of better knowledge nobody can dispute us. So let us say that at some time ages ago, a rough, hairy man made the first picture. Suppose he was trying to explain a certain matter to another primitive man, and because he could not speak except in grunts he resorted to other means to make his intention clear.

51

Speech was not known twelve thousand years ago, we are advised. It is a modern invention. The rough, hairy man was trying to tell the other just where a certain deer would come to water in the evening. He had difficulty. Meat was needed, and for some reason, perhaps domestic, he could not go and desired the other man to go and kill the deer. His speech, which at that time consisted mainly of grunts, was not adequate to describe the location, so finding a spot of smooth sand he made a rough diagram with his finger. This was probably the first picture, and any archaeologist might agree to it. Man had found out that by graphical means he could convey certain ideas to another of his kind.

Beauty was not a part of it, and it was not yet a picture as we see it today. It was but the beginning of the idea. Maybe we are entirely wrong about it, but there is no man who can say that we are. It is as good an explanation as any other.

So at this stage man progressed to the point where he found that certain marks placed in certain ways were useful to convey intentions and meanings. It is not a far reach to where he uses diagrams freely in his daily life, to where he finally makes markings in similitude of some object to show that he means that thing, and to where a man makes a picture that has some elements of arrangement, or composition, and places around it a frame or boundary. This was the first real picture, or pictorial picture. We do not know just what happened, or why it happened. All one can do about this age of picture making is to soliloquize about it to the best of his inventive ability, knowing that, no matter what he says, he is scheduled to bring down upon himself a storm of objections from so-called critics who have entirely different theories. The writer, therefore, has no theories and these thoughts are ventured as possibilities. It does not matter whether we are right or wrong. The point is that once pictures began, and that at first they must have been rough diagrams which gradually were refined to the present day pictures by many processes.

So after all that has been said, we do not really know what prompted man to make his first pictures. Pictures undoubtedly came before words, and as such are better understood. We see the entire history of pictures enacted in children when, with a soft stub of pencil which they alternately chew and make marks with, they begin to make crude hieroglyphics on bits of paper or perhaps the wall. They have this instinct long before they can talk or reason. It is a very primitive thing. Presently we see the child making marks which begin to have some definite design or intention, which shows something comprehensible to us, usually a cat or dog, or some familiar domestic animal. The thing which impresses the child most seems to be something which moves. He understands what he sees better than anything else. His drawings, as we will now call them, get better and one fine day he refines them to the degree that he pencils a frame around one of them. He is now beginning to think, unconsciously, in terms of arrangement or composition. He dimly understands that a picture should have some form of presentation. |Hence the frame.

So now we find the child, and also the primitive man, thinking about their pictures. Boundaries, frames, are created, and they begin to think about what pictures mean and how they should be done. As they progress they find that the frame has an important portion of the burden to bear, and that it makes a difference whether the frame is laid horizontal or vertical. The whole thing takes hold of them, and they begin trying to make pictures of a quality. They find out that one way of doing gives certain impressions and that another gives certain other impressions, so they use these various methods of doing the picture to obtain certain results. A rough texture has a certain effect; a smooth one has another. No matter what is done it has an effect. We find a general refinement of these pictures, and in latter days persons whose sole purpose in life is to talk about them—critics. In the general scale of things, pictures have become so important that a person can demand an existence from the community, and perhaps better, because he is able to say something about them which other men desire to hear. Surely then, pictures are quite an item when this is so, and it is. It is with this idea of their importance that we proceed to discuss them in one little branch, as created by photography.

During the ages that have passed since the first rough diagram was made in the smooth spot of sand,

STUDY IN LINE
Angelo Romano

SUNLIGHT AND SHADOW
Laura Gilpin

man has found out that there are many ways of making pictures. The latest of these, and perhaps the most machine-like is photography, where man literally makes his pictures by means of chemicals, lenses and instruments. Because this has been done in such a mechanical manner, photographic pictures have come under severe criticism from many sources. Many have said that they cannot be pictures, since they are manufactured, as much as sausages are. Others have been more liberal and have been inclined to admit that a picture is a picture regardless of its process; that a photograph can be one as much as an oil painting, admitting at the same time that the oil painting has a standing which the photograph has not, and incidentally that it requires far more training and practice than the latter does. Many painters are very enthusiastic about photography as a pictorial medium, while others say that a good photograph is but a copy of the painting idea. This controversy is not settled yet, and many years will pass before it is. Painting has been recognized and photography has not, and there is always the unfortunate tendency of people to keep the newcomer down until by sheer brute strength, he butts his way into his normal position. So if a photograph is ever recognized as a real picture, it will assuredly deserve it. In the interim we may as well proceed with our work, or our amusement as the case may be, and make our photographs as well as possible, if for no other reason, for the sake of doing good work.

The painters and the pictorial photographers

agree on the one item, that a picture is an important thing. And as pointed out it must be, if a man can be supported by his fellows because they like to read and hear what he has to say about them. A critic is supposed to be able to discuss them intelligently. Generally speaking, he cannot create a picture; he can merely talk about it, and perhaps write. Then surely they, the critics, should be happy to learn that modern invention has at last found a way to make pictures more easily, and in greater quantity, by machinery. It will increase the number of pictures, and their business will be better. They will have more to talk about. But these same critics tell us that this is impossible; that pictures, real pictures that is, cannot be made by machinery or manufactured in quantity. And fortunately they are right, for a real picture is a labor of love. We must create the pictorial photograph, with as much trouble and care as if we were making a painting, even while using a mechanical instrument in its making. Even more as it happens, as we have not the element of color and the charm of texture found in handcraft to assist us in lending to the picture a charm, but must make a picture which has to stand up as such in spite of the fact that we are, to a certain extent, the victims of materials which are manufactured with no regard to their applicability to picture making. In painting there are brushes and colors which are made especially for their use in the craft of painting, whereas in photography there are few manufacturers of materials who even consider the pictorial use of the materials they sell. It is a sad state of affairs.

By all of which, we may say that we are to discuss the making of pictures with an instrument, the camera. We must do all that other pictures do, or as much as the limits of our process will allow, and convey a thought or feeling to others by these pictures, using chemicals for our pigments and lenses for our brushes. It is not our business to argue whether a photograph stands equal as a work of art beside paintings and other pictures, or even to discuss art in any sense. Our business here is to say certain things which affect the picture value of a photograph, and to let the photograph stand on its own value as the worker sees it. There are many serious workers in pictorial photography. They make the picture to hang on the wall as meritorious of itself, regardless of the subject matter, and it is supposed to have a value aside from that of pure record. These many persons have agreed unanimously that the photograph has a just reason to be classed among the arts, and that a good picture can be made with the camera. We must accept the verdict of many minds, whether we agree or not. We, too, then, must stand behind the statement that a photograph has a value as a picture, aside from that of mere reproduction. A photograph can be a picture as well as an oil painting or an etching. Whether it can ever be a great picture, to hang on the walls of the Museum, we are not prepared to say. We think not, but are contradicted by Clarence White, and he is a man who has spent a lifetime teaching the thought of making good photographs which have an art value. Probably he knows more about it, and he is emphatic in saying that a photograph has a value that entitles it to hang in the great museum, housed with paintings by great masters, and classic sculptures. Maybe he is right; he has thought a great deal about it, and it is not impossible. Let us say that it is possible, and that a great photograph can be made; one that will one day hang in the Museum, so that people five hundred years from now will stop in front of it and discuss it, and argue about it; so that the papers of that time will print things about it as an important item in the life of the period, as they now do about the Rembrandts and Whistlers. It is possible, and what we are supposed to do is to go into the thoughts and ways that will assist the pictorial worker in progressing to the point where he might be able to create such a picture, were such a phenomenon possible. We do not even whisper that it is possible, it being mentioned as the possible goal of the pictorial worker if he cares to aim high.

TEA POT
Mercedes Desmore

MISSION CHURCH—LAGUNA
Forman Hanna

CHAPTER III.

HISTORY OF PICTORIAL PHOTOGRAPHY

PICTORIAL photography, in name and fact, belongs to our own time. We cannot find the term in use before 1890. There was, to be sure, much said and written during the earlier fifty years about Art in photography. Right at the beginning of things, Arago, in his first announcement of the Daguerreotype process in 1839, startled the world with the famous but false prophecy: "Painting is doomed." It was a false start and ended, as it deserved, in failure.

During its first half-century, the development of photography was almost wholly along technical and mechanical lines. Those who followed its practise, professional and amateur alike, were engrossed by its unrivalled capacity as a method of reproduction, and technical excellence was the supreme standard of quality. There were, of course, exceptions. D. O. Hill, a Scots painter who used the Colotype process of Talbot as early as 1843, Mrs. Cameron and Rejlander who followed him, and others whose names are forgotten, have left us examples of pictorial photography quite as interesting as anything produced today. So, as early as 1869, H. P. Robinson, an English professional, published his "Pictorial Effect in Photography," which, with his work of the twenty years following, enjoyed a worldwide popularity—and so on. But these were isolated and sporadic appearances.

It was not until the eighties, when photography had been enormously simplified, when the modern amateur arrived and photographic societies multiplied like flies in summertime, that there was any glimmering of the use of photography as a means of individual expression and what today we call "pictorial photography" came up over the horizon.

It was the beginning of a new day and arose, here and abroad, in the discontent of an increasing number of serious amateurs with the inanity of the "snapshot" and the coldly mechanical perfection of the record-photograph of the time. The first efforts of the new school workers to exploit the use of the camera as a means of individual expression met with universal opposition and contempt. This opposition, and the failure of the judges of the photographic exhibitions of the day to recognize the merit of the work of the new school, led to organization on the part of the new school men—and the fight for the recognition of pictorial photography was on.

The pictorial movement, as a definite and concerted thing, began, let us say, at the International Exposition at Vienna in 1891. There, for the first time, the work of several English "pictorialists" was recognized with praise as a distinct advance in photography. Among those attracted by that work were two members of the Vienna Camera Club—Hans Watzek and Hugo Henneberg—who later associated themselves with Heinrich Kuehn and Dr.

Spitzer in a systematic investigation of the possibilities of photography as a medium of pictorial
expression. These were the pioneers of the Viennese
school of pictorialists who, with the Hofmeister
brothers of Hamburg, firmly established the cult
of pictorial photography in Austria and Germany.

Encouraged by their success at Vienna, and smart-
ing under the treatment accorded them at the exhibitions of the Photographic Society (now the R.
P. S.), London, a few English workers, led by H.
P. Robinson, Alfred Maskell, A. Horsley Hinton
and two or three others, organized The Linked Ring
(1892) and in 1893 held the first Photographic Salon
(London) where, for the first time in the history
of photographic exhibitions, (1) no awards were
offered, (2) the photographs submitted were judged
by a committee of photographers, and (3) only
photographs showing distinct artistic merit were accepted and hung. The success of this Salon, and the
strenuous opposition and comment it aroused, gave
shape and purpose to the pictorial movement in
England. The membership of The Linked Ring
grew in numbers and influence, and acceptance at
the London Salons was regarded as the "blue ribbon"
of the pictorial field.

In the following year (1894) the Photo Club of
Paris held its first Photographic Salon, gathering
into a group the scattered and isolated pictorialists
of Paris: Demachy, le Begue, Puyo, Dubreuil and
others. The influence of this group quickly spread
to the larger cities of France and resulted in a new

enthusiasm for photography. Similarly the pictorial movement made its way into Belgium, Italy, Russia and Holland, everywhere infusing new life and spirit into photography.

In America, as in England, the birth and development of pictorial photograhy was attended by persistent opposition and controversy. The work of the new school, wherever exhibited, was received with condemnation and contempt. In vain did pictorialists endeavor to secure a fair or favorable judgment of their work, on the score of artistic merit, from judges whose standards of excellence were "definition, light and shade and chemical effects." Many advanced amateurs therefore sought at European exhibitions the recognition they were denied at home.

Among these advanced amateurs, about 1894, appeared Alfred Stieglitz, who had studied photography under Vogel at Berlin and was familiar with the beginnings of pictorial photography in Europe. Blessed with wealth, leisure and an untiring energy, and animated by the single purpose of advancing photography in its application as a means of individual expression, Stieglitz, first as editor of "The American Amateur Photographer" and later as editor of "Camera Notes," the organ of the Camera Club of New York, gathered around him a company of enthusiastic workers of the new school, whose activities, photographic and propagandic, he directed with masterly skill. The volumes of "Camera Notes" for 1897-1901 are filled with the record of these remarkable activities and the opposition they

ADORATION
R. W. Trowbridge

APPLES

P. J. Schweickart

called forth. Under Stieglitz's direction and influence the pictorial movement in America made extraordinary progress and the work of the New American School, as it was called, attracted worldwide attention. Among the workers of this school may be recalled the names of F. Holland Day, Gertrude Kasebier, Alvin Langdon Coburn, Eugene, Steichen, Eickemeyer, Fraser, Berg, Keiley and Clarence H. White. In 1896 a Salon, modeled upon that of London, was held at Washington. It was followed by the Philadelphia Salons of 1898-1900, New York 1899, and an important exhibition of the work of Alfred Stieglitz in the same year, the Chicago Salon of 1900, with other exhibitions at New York, Philadelphia and San Francisco following. In 1901 F. Holland Day showed in London an important collection of American pictorial work, which largely added to the prestige of the American School.

In 1902 Stieglitz and his associates organized The Photo Secession, a group of pictorial workers resembling The Linked Ring in purpose and scope, the members of which held an exhibition of their work at the National Arts Club, New York, during the same year. This was followed in 1903 by the establishment of "Camera Work," a sumptuous quarterly which represented The Photo Secession and was the mouthpiece of the movement during the following ten or twelve years. In 1905 the Little Galleries of the Photo Secession were opened at 291 Fifth Avenue, New York. During the nineties the work of the Secession was shown by invitation at all the important exhibitions held here and abroad, at Pittsburg, Chicago, Cincinnati, San Francisco, Berlin, Dresden, Vienna, St. Petersburg, Paris, London, Brussels, Turin, Glasgow and a hundred other towns, the culmination of the Secession's achievement being reached at the Buffalo exhibition of 1910, when a collection of photographs was shown in the Albright Art Galleries of that City.

From the date of the Buffalo exhibition, the photographic activities of The Photo-Secession seemed to decline and the Pittsburgh Salon, organized in 1910, the Photo-Pictorialists of Buffalo, with the Photographic Guild of Baltimore and many similar groups came into prominence. In 1916 the National Institute of Graphic Arts gave an exhibition at New York, showing the evolution of photography from its beginning in 1839 to 1916, giving especial prominence to the development of pictorial photography. This led to the organization of The Pictorial Photographers of America, under the leadership of Clarence H. White, for the purpose of stimulating the popular interest in pictorial photography. The activities of this organization, national in scope and closely allied with other groups of workers in arts and crafts, have resulted in a widespread revival of the old-time enthusiasm among American pictorial photographers. Collections of photographs have been made and routed throughout the principal cities of the Union; an "Annual" has been published giving reproductions of the best photographic work of the year, co-operation has been given to the various Salons now established in several of the larger cities, and a Gallery, with a meeting room for visiting pictorialists, has been established as part of the New York Art Centre. The exhibitions of the P. P. of A. have been notable for the quality of the work shown and the International Salon, held at New York during May, 1923, recalled the glories of past years.

CHAPTER IV.

MATERIALS, APPARATUS AND TECHNIQUE

IN Pictorial Photography one should have his technique developed to a point where it can be laid aside as of no worry, in order to concentrate upon the important item of getting the picture. One must not be molested with thoughts about exposure and mechanisms, as they are very diverting and interfere with the work. Technique must be so good that it is no trouble, and the real pictorial worker should be a far better straight photographer than any professional, which is not usually the case. There are those in photography who have a house full of cameras and lenses, and buy everything which comes out for the sheer pleasure of having new toys to play with. These gentlemen we will take heed of to the extent of doing precisely the opposite of what they do. We set them aside as very promising fellows who may one day invent a new shutter or do something for the mechanical side of photography. Every man has his use.

The pictorialist is warned not to become confused with mechanisms, and to keep his equipment and processes as simple as possible as one of the greatest steps toward doing good work. We do not say that he should stand satisfied with some old view camera with a three dollar lens, made several years before photography was invented in its modern sense. This would be quite as bad as becoming involved in too much machinery. In all things there is a happy medium and, while we would suggest avoiding intricacy, it is well that the worker should be properly equipped, remembering that no matter what the expense, it is justified if it adds to his comfort in working.

There are a great many pictorial workers who have so successfully evaded the technical side of photography that, unless they turn back and learn something about proper chemicals and equipment, their further progress is barred. Then there are those good technicians who cannot see a picture. Something of both technician and artist is demanded of the real pictorialist, his technique being so perfect that he uses it without thought, free to give his entire attention to the work of making the picture.

There are those who have used stock developers for so long that they have become ignorant of the chemistry of photography, until they find that they cannot proceed to new accomplishments. They perhaps have used them for so long that they fail to think of them as developers and have fallen into a lazy ignorance knowing that the bottle is always ready so long as they have a dollar to buy it with. These will never become good photographic workers.

The new worker should spend his first months in learning to make a good straight sharp negative. Doubtless he has some friend, a professional photographer, who will advise him. The commercial photographer would probably recommend a nega-

73

tive too strong for pictorial work, and it is well to take his advice with reserve. The portrait photographer is more likely to have a correct thought about negative density for the pictorialist, which would be quite useful, since he has had to make a study of gradation in his work. There is really no way of telling just what proper density is, and one can go into endless description and yet convey no meaning. Perhaps it is best to say that the proper negative for the pictorial worker is one in which the greatest density, or sky portion, is so thin that it is possible to read a newspaper through it in a good light. It should at the same time, have enough deposit in the shadows to insure detail in that portion. This will do to get started on, and the worker can refine it to the correct point as he finds what his requirements are.

As said, the best way to get started is to ask some professional photographer. He has to make a living out of the work and has some standards whereas the average amateur for a long time has none, and makes the muddiest kind of negatives. Once having made a negative which he considers good, adjust the density down, usually to a point where it is possible to make a good pictorial print. A thin negative is best, of course, unless so thin that it is impossible to obtain a good print from it, and even then it is better than a hard, thick negative, as a little intensification will snap it up so that it will work well. The typical thin, fogged, muddy, negative of the average amateur worker is not included in this description, as it should never be used at all.

The business of learning to make a good, clean, sharp negative will take some time, perhaps months, and the worker is strongly advised against going deeper into photography until he has learned to do this one thing. It is the basis of all future work. No matter what he does in future years, he will always have to rest his entire efforts upon the negative, and he must know this part of it thoroughly. It is impossible for him to venture into soft focus work until he has first learned to make a good, sharp negative. When this is accomplished, it is well to turn to the soft focus lens, and it will be found that the problem of development will have to be worked out all over again, as it is quite another matter. In the developer, the negative made with the soft focus lens seems to fog all over, the worker being inclined to "pull" the plate when it goes black. The resulting negative is thin and muddy and it is impossible to do much with it, whereas had it been left in the developer longer it would have been all right. Some workers develop the soft focus negative until they see the image through on the back of the plate, using a standard double-coated plate. This is really a rule of thumb method of development and in using it a worker automatically admits that he is a bad technician, or he would know how to develop without such a primitive guide. Incidentally, the better grade of double-coated plates are coated so heavily that if one should develop until the image showed through the back, the negative would be so dense that it could not be printed. The only way to judge density in development, aside from the time temperature method, is to do so by estimating the density, and to keep at it until no matter what plate is used the worker will know what is going on when it is in the developer. We must learn by a process of failure, in all things that we do.

A schedule of the proper steps for the embryo worker to follow, is inserted as a help for him, in order that he may not venture into the more complicated processes first.

1. Making the sharp negative.
2. Contact printing from the sharp negative.
3. The portrait negative, nearly sharp, or sharp.
4. Printing the portrait negative.
5. The soft focus negative.
6. Contact printing from the soft focus negative.
7. Enlarging on bromide and fast chloride papers.
8. The enlarged negative, on glass and paper.
9. The platinum and palladium print. (Also kallitype).
10. The gum print. The gum platinum print.
11. The oil and bromoil print, and oil transfer.

If the worker will follow the above schedule, and never leave the one process until he has become skillful at it, no matter how long it takes, in a period of time he should be ready for serious pictorial work. It is not necessary that he should ever have to pass beyond bromide printing and enlarging in order to be considered a good worker. A good print on

CALIFORNIA LANDSCAPE
Fred R. Dapprich

DANCERS
Edwin Gore Dunning

bromide is far better than a bad one on platinum. The picture is the thing, not the print, and that is all settled when the negative is made. This little fact has not yet penetrated the minds of about ninety percent of our best pictorial workers, who will persist in making a few bad negatives a year, and spending the rest of their time in the darkroom trying by terrible efforts and some intricate printing process, to get from them a good print. The pictorialist should first learn to operate a camera. Many times exhibition juries have passed bad pictures because they were beautifully printed, and discarded good ones simply because they were improperly finished, whereas they might very well have done just the reverse and have done more to encourage good photography. The print in some cases is just a disguise, a make-up so to speak, to cover up the many other deficiencies in the picture, and curiously enough, the average man is entirely opaque to this very evident trick of pictorialists. A plain commercial photograph of a tomato can can be so beautifully printed that it looks well, and that seems to be the present day standard of judgment, an ulcer which has been thrust upon photography by the platinum printing of the just passed generation of pictorialists.

We are concerned with the simplification of technique as one of the greatest helps to the pictorialist. As a help toward this end it is suggested that he never go beyond his ability or venture into strange byways where he will get into trouble. This one sentence should be written a thousand times, and every beginner forced to read it ten times over, until he even mumbles it in his sleep. It must be learned, or there will be trouble. The business of the pictorialist is to make pictures, and when he has exposed the negative the work is ninety percent done, the rest being sure knowledge of his medium. If he chooses to dabble in chemical processes, he can very well remember that he is satisfying his curiosity in a chemical and not in a pictorial direction.

CAMERAS

As to cameras there are so many kinds applicable to pictorial work that it is almost safe to say that anything but an engraver's camera will do. All are good, according to what one is doing, from the miniature camera to the 8 x 10 view. A few words may not be wasted in brief description.

Starting with the smallest, since there seems to be no logical sequence, the miniature camera has many advantages. But so have all the others, as it happens. It, however, has the especial advantage that it is more likely to be with the worker when an opportunity comes to make a picture, and many of our leading workers have lately taken to this method of making their negatives. The truth is that they change from type to type with clockwork regularity and usually end up with the reflecting camera. However, the miniature camera has the advantage of being small and light. How many times have we heard, "If I only had the camera with me this minute." That is the greatest virtue of the small camera. Fitted with a fast lens, usually an f 4.5 anastigmat, set normally at infinity, it has a great range.

There is very little trouble in getting well-exposed sharp negatives. The small lens is said to allow more light to pass than a larger lens of the same f speed, on account of the very small amount of glass in it. While this is a common assertion among motion picture operators, one should not count upon the point to get proper exposure, and it will not add any properties to the lens when it really gets dark. The negative used in these cameras is about 1⅝ by 2¼, and must be enlarged either directly on bromide or chloride paper, or by making an enlarged negative. It is too small to be used in contact printing. The direct print made by enlargement is usually a little softened on account of printing, and looks very well. If the negative has been kept thin, the wiry definition is not very noticeable, it being a curious fact that definition depends upon contrast in order that it be visible, and a soft print will not appear nearly so sharp as one which is contrasty. If diffusion is desired it is best to make an enlarged negative, making the positive sharp and softening the final negative.

The next larger camera for the consideration of the pictorial worker is the 6½ x 9 centimeter or 2½ x 3½, usually of foreign make. While the miniature camera just mentioned requires practically no focusing, on account of its short focus lens, the 6½ x 9 centimeter requires more careful attention to this point of operation, since it usually has a fast anastigmat of about 4 in. focus. It is heavier and makes a negative which will stand considerable enlargement, up to 11 x 14 if desired, provided there are no imperfections in it. A small pinhole is not so objectionable on a plate of this size, as it can generally be worked out and a good print obtained, whereas with the miniature camera a pinhole spells trouble, on account of the fact that it is multiplied by enlargement.

The quarter plate, or $3\frac{1}{4}$ x $4\frac{1}{4}$ folding type camera is still more useful in doing good work, but has the disadvantage of added weight, and requires still more careful adjustment. These cameras are usually of the folding plate type, the serious worker seldom using a roll film camera, since it is not flexible enough in operation. This camera has a focusing back which slides into place, and is surer in its working, where careful adjustment and control of arrangement is desired. It can be used with tripod, making a small view camera if desired.

The most popular camera used by the pictorial worker is the reflex, with perhaps a soft focus lens, or one which has a device for diffusion. Of the three sizes, $2\frac{1}{4}$ x $3\frac{1}{4}$, $3\frac{1}{4}$ x $4\frac{1}{4}$, and 4 x 5, the $3\frac{1}{4}$ x $4\frac{1}{4}$ seems to be the favorite, fitted with a lens ranging from 7″ to 10″ in focus. These cameras are fitted with revolving back, rising front, and other adjustments and are a great pleasure to work with, permitting a great range of use. In fact, any work can be done with this type of camera, except

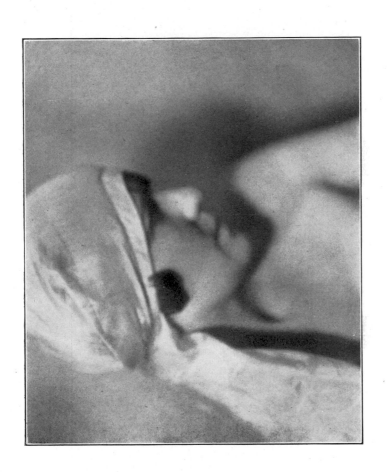

PORTRAIT
A. P. Milne

THE HUSBANDMAN

O. C. Reiter

perhaps, wide angle pictures. The shutter being
focal plane is very efficient, and permits the use of
lenses at smaller stops than any other shutter, this
being an advantage in the control of depth and
definition.

In purchasing a camera of this sort the worker is
urged to see that he gets one with all possible adjustments, except perhaps, the swing front which is
practically useless, and of little advantage where
lenses of large openings are to be used, except in
portrait work. The reversible or revolving back is
a great advantage and absolutely necessary, with the
preference lying with the latter. The rising front
is also a requirement, and good work cannot be done
without it. The advantage in all cases lies with the
foreign cameras as they have a refinement of adjustment and mechanism which makes them better to
work with. On the other hand, they are not so sturdy
and will get out of order far easier, while the American cameras will stand for much abuse. So the idea
is that if one desires a camera to stand hard knocks
he should get the American instrument, and if fine
work is desired, with care to be taken of the instrument, get the foreign camera.

Many prefer view cameras, using tripod in their
work. This does not permit great flexibility of travel,
and is cumbersome, but on the other hand the view
camera has certain advantages over any other, being
much better than any for portrait work except, perhaps, the large studio cameras which cannot be
transported outside the house. They are obtainable

in 4 x 5, 5 x 7, 6½ x 8½, 8 x 10 sizes, and 11 x 14 if desired, but the last is entirely too large for any ordinary purpose, and very heavy.

The 4 x 5 view camera has become very popular for beginners, principally on account of its light weight and low cost of operation, since many failures do not become expensive. It requires enlargement, of course. The 5 x 7 has many advantages, being large enough for small contact printing, and permitting the worker to have many additions to his equipment all in the one case. In one instance a serious pictorialist had a special leather case built to hold the camera, tripod, eighteen plateholders, seven lenses, and various other equipment, including a shutter which was so built that it would take any one of the lenses, all of which were in barrel. The 6½ x 8½ and 8 x 10 cameras are also very popular instruments, and when the photographer is quite sure about what he desires and also about his technique, these are perhaps the best of all cameras. It is, however, no use to carry such a weight if the worker is not sure that he is going to be able to make a good negative, or if not sure about the picture he is going to make. In this way these sizes are perhaps an incentive to good work, as one is more careful and thinks his picture out before he makes it, knowing the hard work involved. Contact prints are made, and when all is written there is none so fine as the contact print, in any one of the many papers which may be used.

LENSES

From what has been said about cameras it may be gathered that almost any lens will answer for making a good picture, providing that the user knows what it will do and what its limitations are. The main thing is that the lens should be properly handled.

The small cameras are necessarily fitted with fast, short focus anastigmat lenses which cut very sharply and require practically no focusing on account of their extreme depth. These are the only lenses which do not require careful focusing.

The modern anastigmats manufactured by good makers have, of course, a very flat field giving unusually even definition all over the plate and critical definition wide open. This is generally true of the smaller sizes, they being far easier to correct than the larger lenses and having far better definition. On the other hand, it is a curious fact that there are very few f 4.5 anastigmats in the longer foci, from 6″ up, which give a perfectly flat field and critical definition wide open, although all are advertised that they do. There are also some lenses which are advertised that they give a fine softened quality when used wide open, f 4.5, whereas they simply have failed to get their full corrections and choose to make of this a selling point. An anastigmat should cut critically sharp wide open, if it deserves to be called an anastigmat, and should have a flat field to cover the plate evenly. If a lens does not equal these requirements it is not a good lens, as an anastigmat. The new worker is advised, if he desires to purchase this type of lens, to ask the advice of some experienced professional about whether the lens is good or bad before he pays his money for a so-called fast anastigmat.

The process lens is a super corrected anastigmat with far flatter field and better color corrections, usually working at f 8.0. It is used by photo-engravers who require microscopic definition and is not a lens which might interest the pictorial worker. Even these lenses, while made at f 8.0, are operated at small f stops and will not give microscopic definition at the f 8.0 stop. So it follows that what we are inclined to call needle sharp is not so sharp as we think but only appears to be so. Nearly every anastigmat when used wide open, at f 4.5, shows an appreciable loss in definition from the center to the edges of the plate, visible when the negative is subjected to a magnifying glass. The grain of the plate, however, is not fine enough to take care of this slight change due to distortion and consequently it makes no great difference. The process lens is capable of making images which are so microscopically sharp that they cannot be registered upon the ordinary dry plate at all on account of the grain.

Perhaps one of the best lenses which the pictorial worker can select for general purposes is the ordinary rapid rectilinear, working at f 8.0. It makes a picture fairly sharp, but not of so wiry a quality as the anastigmat, and so is less difficult to handle in

CHEMICALS
Paul Outerbridge, Jr.

NOVEMBER MIST
Fred M. Doudna

pictorial work. This lens, however, is quite slow, as judged by modern standards, although plenty fast enough for outdoor work. It has poor covering power, and gives an uneven quality of definition unless a fairly long focus lens is used, say one which equals in focus the sum of the sides of the plate. For a 5 x 7 plate we would select a 12″ to 14″ lens. Even then there is a visible loss in quality from the center to the sides. In using a rectilinear we find out many things about it by association, that we would not by first test. This is true of any lens. Stopped down it appears to make a fairly sharp picture, but not so sharp as the anastigmat. If we should make a negative with the rectilinear and then enlarge it to a three time linear dimension, using the same lens, we will speedily see that it is very deficient in definition. This, however, is more of an advantage than a trouble in pictorial work, as we try to avoid needle sharp pictures.

Actual definition and apparent definition are two entirely different things. It appears that definition, that is apparent definition, is not altogether a matter of lens quality and that, if we use a lens which makes a very sharp image, we can still, by soft negative development, get a very fine print which is not objectionable. Whereas we can take an ordinary rectilinear and, by strong development, make a contrasty negative which will give a print that will look very sharp, even when it is not sharp. This is a very important factor in pictorial work and one which must be thoroughly digested, as it will give the worker a control over his rendition of line values and vastly improve the general quality of his pictures.

We next come to the soft focus lens, which every pictorialist should master if he wishes to make pictures which are lovely to look upon. With the use of the soft focus lens there is a fine softening of detail which pulls the whole picture together and adds a tone value not obtainable with any other lens. The user is not advised to take advantage of the extreme diffusion possible with this lens, or to make pictures which are so mushy that it is difficult to tell what they are all about. This is the extreme which spoils everything and brings down criticism upon the so-called artistic worker. While the soft focus lens has been the one great addition to pictorial photography in the last twenty years, it has at the same time been a handicap to good work in the sense that so many unsophisticated amateurs have run wild making pictures under the assumption that anything fuzzy is pictorial. Anything which can do good also has the power to do harm, and this is an instance. There is also the good soul who likes to shock people with his knowledge, not knowing fully himself. He makes a very wooly picture and tells his friends who know nothing about it, that this is the "new art" in photography. Perhaps he believes it himself. It does a great lot of harm however, the good workers having to suffer for it and stand the loss of good will and opinion that goes with such foolishness.

92

The minute some people develop any art sense they seem to think they are of the immortals and can do as they please. When we come to soft focus lenses we immediately encounter insanity. These so-called artistic photographers, who know little of composition and less of picture making except that they have a soft focus lens, seem to take a vicious delight in shocking people in general. It is the curse of small knowledge. They think themselves little Bernard Shaws. The one who has a small glimmering of the fact that he can see things as other men cannot, takes an arrogant advantage of the fact and deliberately presents his thoughts, whether pictorial or otherwise, in a manner which he secretly hopes will not be understood. Not being understood he is artistic. This is the embryo's manner of thinking, but as he gets older and more tolerant he sees that it is better to keep within reach of as many people as possible for only in that way can we progress to better things.

But to return to the soft focus lens. Of these lenses there are many kinds, singles, doublets, convertibles, and one which has an adjustment for diffusion and can be a full-blooded anastigmat when occasion demands. The single lens is very fine to work with but unless a very long focus is used, perhaps twice the long side of the plate, it lacks in covering power. This does not matter in certain cases, but is essential to really fine even work. Stop for stop, the single lens is faster than any lens made. In the same thought, stop for stop, no lens is faster than any lens, and the single lens being closer to no lens at all, the simplest and has the least glass to be reckoned with, also the least corrections, it is the fastest. For a 5 x 7 plate it would be well to use a 14″ lens if even quality is desired. In the single lenses the chemical and visual images do not coincide and it is necessary to allow for this change in focusing. This is due to lack of color correction.

The soft focus doublet is a better lens to work with, and some of them are now being built so that the rear element is a single lens of about 50% longer focus, and corrected for use as such. This is more simple to work with, since the color correction is better and the necessity of allowing for change of focus is avoided. It also has a better quality of drawing for the same reason. There has been a tendency of late years to work more firmly, and leave aside the wooly pictures so prevalent some years ago. These lenses are so built that they give a good usable quality at comparatively wide openings, the fastest working at f 4.0. None of the soft focus lenses has a flat field as compared with anastigmats, but a slight change is not noticeable when the definition is diffused. The definition varies from the center to the edges of the plate to a considerable degree and, unless a long focus lens is used, which minimizes this defect, it becomes apparent. A lens of about one and one-half the diagonal of the plate should be selected for good covering power.

There is one lens which gives a very fine diffused quality quite different from the soft focus lenses men-

94

tioned above. It has an adjustable ring which controls the position of the front element, moving it in and out. This controls the diffusion and, unlike any soft focus lens, the diffusion does not depend upon the adjustment of the diaphragm. Whereas in the soft focus lenses it becomes necessary to stop down to get firmer quality, with loss of speed, any diffusion desired in this lens may be obtained at the full aperture by adjustment of the front ring, making it invaluable in portrait work. It can also be used the same as any soft focus lens by setting the front ring for full diffusion and using the diaphragm for control. The problem of halo has also been solved and it gives a greater diffusion than any lens without the troublesome run-around so objectionable in soft focus lenses improperly used. Incidentally, it has a flat field and is an anastigmat when adjusted for sharp.

As to focus of lens required in pictorial work, this is a matter which is totally one of opinion. A picture is a picture whether it is made with a wide angle lens or otherwise. It has been generally recommended that the worker use a focus of the same length as the sum of the sides of the plate. For instance, using a 4 x 5 plate, a 9″ lens would be selected. The long focus narrow angle lens is most assuredly the easiest to keep out of trouble with and, since it includes less, it will make pictures which are simpler, and being so are easier to handle in arrangement. The idea is presented that if one cannot get the picture on the plate with the long focus lens and should have no other lens along, the picture is lost; whereas if a wider angle, shorter focus lens is used, the worker will stand a better chance of getting all subject matter on the plate. If a portion of the plate be used afterward, and that portion is enlarged, he has the same result as a long focus lens. This is the most flexible manner of working but necessitates enlargement and cutting out portions of the plate, which makes arrangement difficult. It is far better to have the boundaries of the picture space to work to, as only in that way can one get compositions which are delicately balanced.

As to convertible lenses, these are anastigmats ranging in speed from f 6.3 to f 7.7. A 7 3/16" lens would have a back element of about 11½", and a front element of about 14". The single lenses are corrected to give sharp pictures at the full opening, f 12.5, and are very useful in landscape work or any work where there are no straight lines to worry about. They are not useful in architectural photography as the single elements give bowed lines, convex or concave, due to barrel distortion, which cannot be avoided in this type of lens. They are very useful, however, for general work and the curving of the lines when the single elements are used is no fault of the maker,—it is found in all single lenses where the cell is placed at one end of the barrel.

PLATES AND FILMS

The roll film is seldom found in pictorial work since it is used mainly in cameras which have no focusing device. It is not discussed for that reason.

The cut films are made for use in plateholders and are a great help as they reduce the load of the traveler, especially in the larger sizes, being much lighter than plates. The film is made in two speeds, fast and extra fast, and in a slower orthochromatic emulsion. The ordinary emulsion is orthochromatic only inasmuch as it has a yellowish cast of itself and is coated upon celluloid, which gives it a slight sensitiveness to the yellows. It is so slightly sensitive to the yellow however, that a filter has practically no effect. The film has a very soft emulsion, good for portrait work, and holds it softness even under prolonged development. It is troublesome in development and the danger of marring the surface is great. In printing also it is rather more difficult to handle, in contact printing having a tendency to lose contact unless under severe pressure, and in enlargement not lying flat in the kit unless held in place by two sheets of glass. So the great advantage of the film in pictorial work is lightness.

The same emulsion as we have on the film, coated on a glass plate, will make a faster plate. This is a statement commonly made among workers who really know, and seldom do we find the news photographer using anything but plates in spite of their weight. Speed is not so much of an advantage as quality of emulsion, however, and in that respect plates excel greatly.

Plates are made in all emulsions, the ordinary which is sensitive to blue only, the orthochromatic which is sensitive to yellow as well as blue, and the panchromatic which is sensitive to red, yellow and blue. Plates are called by many names, some of them more or less confusing, and the worker will have to wade through the maze of Isos, Orthos, Panchros, and other names to his own selections.

The orthochromatic plate, while sensitive to yellow as well as blue, allows the blue light to record faster. If a proper value of both colors is desired, one will have to use a yellow filter which retards all colors but yellow and allows it to record fully, thus bringing the blues and yellows into their proper relation. The blue light is held back while the yellow does its work. The deeper the yellow of the filter the more the blue light is held back. This is based upon the fact that the orthochromatic plate is sensitive to but two colors, blue and yellow.

The panchromatic plate is sensitive to red, yellow and blue, but the colors do not record in their true monochromatic values, filters being used to get proper values. Sometimes values are taken untruthfully to get certain results, and this fact is brought to the attention of the worker that he may study it more fully.

Plates are made in all speeds and all degrees of contrast, as well as varying color sensitiveness. From the contrast plate for making reproductions of line drawings to the high speed plates we have many to select from, but it is well for the pictorial worker to stick to few kinds and learn those well in order to avoid trouble. For ordinary pictorial work the

TWO FANS
Mercedes Desmore

NUREMBURG

Arthur James Deering

double coated orthochromatic plate is best. It is a plate with a fast ortho top emulsion, and an under emulsion which is slower. This gives it the property of recording good tone values over a wide range of contrast. Its non-halation properties are a factor but not so much as the former, which is the important thing in pictorial photography.

There are quite a number of brands upon the market, varying in quality, and the worker is to find the one he thinks best. The plate which has an under coating sensitive to yellow also ought to be the best of all, and perhaps it might also have a greater ratio of speed between the top and under coatings. Thickness of coating is also a factor in pictorial work, which may be speedily discovered by the fact that such a plate fixes more slowly. It is well for the worker to try every kind of double-coated plate and find the one which most nearly approaches this specification, and that will be the best for pictorial work.

For portraiture the double-coated plate has a tendency to block up in the highlights, especially if there is under exposure. A single-coated plate is best for this work, one which is medium fast. The extremely fast emulsions never have the quality of the medium emulsions. Whether an ordinary blue sensitive plate is used or a single-coated, fast ortho plate, makes no great difference if the worker knows his development well, either one being good for the purpose. The advanced amateurs have a tendency to use the ortho while all the professionals use the fast ordinary plate. And the amateurs do not seem to make very good portraits, which seems to prove that the man is superior to his medium if he knows his work.

THE EXPOSURE OF THE PLATE

Tone values which are so important in photography can only be thought of in terms of exposure, for only in that way can they be controlled. The whole picture, even as to structure, depends upon the proper rendition of values, and a mass can be accented or subdued as desired if exposure is controlled. Even in the control processes, bromoil, oil, gum and the like, proper tone values must be regulated in the negative in order that they shall appear properly on the final print. If they are not right or good, no inking or brush work will correct them. This is a great argument in favor of the straight print but, of course, there are many things to be said for the manipulation printing processes.

So there is no such thing as correct exposure and all exposure meters are foolish. While they are made with good intent, the makers laboring under the error that there is such a thing as correct exposure, they are only misleading in this work or, in fact, in any photographic work except perhaps in photo-engraving where the process is purely technical and is done under artificial light in every circumstance, and there they are not used.

Since the object of the worker is to get a picture which he makes by photography, the principal thing to be considered is the rendering of values such as will record the worker's ideas as he sees them. This cannot be disputed. Under those circumstances the photographer must regulate the exposure so that it will do this. If what is called correct exposure will do it, then he is to use it. If under-exposure, so-called, will get him an effect which he desires, then it becomes correct exposure; and if over-exposure will do certain things which he wishes, then that too is correct exposure. In sum, the correct exposure is that which will make a negative to print as the photographer desires, and that is the only correct exposure. In many cases a severely short exposure is the best, and in many others a very long exposure. We cannot truthfully refer to under and over-exposure, for there are no such things in real photographic work.

We sometimes desire a soft result and, in such a case, we cannot help but use a long exposure. Sometimes we require a contrasty result, and then we must use a short exposure. We encounter a subject on a clear sunny day where the shadows are deep, the highlights or sunny portions being very bright and, while all the items in our picture are as we would have them, they do not seem to pull together on account of the spotty character of the lighting. This can be regulated by very full exposure, and a development which will pull all these items together in the manner that will produce a better feeling of unity. We also come to the situation where we have a very fine pictorial thought for our camera and find that the lighting is flat and uninteresting and that the picture would be better off if it were more vigorous or if we had some sunshine to deal with. In such cases it is very easy to cut exposure in such a manner that we can obtain an effect which is desirable.

So it seems that, disregarding the light to a certain extent, exposure in this work should be made with regard to what contrasts are wanted, more being given as we wish soft prints with values well held together, and less being used as we wish contrasts. Development will take care of many deficiencies.

DEVELOPERS

There is a deplorable tendency to use the ready bottled developers in pictorial work and very soon the worker will know nothing about the chemistry of photography if he follows this road. This developer is quite a good one, non-staining, and makes a blue-black deposit of silver requiring a rather full development to get a good printing negative. It is usually made in highly concentrated form, being mixed with from ten to sixty parts of water for use. Being a single reagent developer, it renders a true scale of values and is useful in color separation work where this is a requirement. The developer made up of two reducing agents does not render a true scale of gradation, since one agent reduces before the other and a broken scale results. So it cannot be used for color work. This is brought up, as any real work should have a true scale of gradation, and if the developer will stand the test of color

GATE IN GARDEN OF MAXFIELD PARRISH
Clara E. Sipprell

OLD PRAGUE
Dr. D. J. Ruzicka

separation it will do anything else. The two solution developers will not do this, although they might answer for ordinary purposes.

While the Paramidophenol Hydrochloride developers are very fine non-staining single reagent developers, the worker should know what they consist of in order to appreciate fully how they work, and the formula is given herewith so that they may be readily made up by anybody.

Water .... 1000 parts by weight
Paramidophenol Hydro-
    chloride .... 100 "   "   "
Soda Sulphite (dry) ...... 300 "   "   "

Boil the above ten minutes.

Add saturated solution Caustic Soda, which will form a precipitate.

Add more slowly, stirring until precipitate dissolves and clears, and no more.

When cool this gives the concentrated developer.

For use   1 to 20
                    1 to 40
                    1 to 60
For contrast use 1 to 10.

Metol may also be used in the above and is even better since it does not precipitate.

The three-solution Pyro Developer is just as good however, and far more flexible in use. For those who do not know it, it is given as one which will answer all purposes.

A. Water .... 16 oz.
    Oxalic Acid .... 20 grains
    Pyro .... 1 oz.
B. Water .... 16 oz.
    Dry Soda Sulphite ...... 2 oz.
C. Water .... 16 oz.
    Dry Carbonate Soda .... 1 oz.

For use. 1 A, 1 B, 1 C, 6 to 8 water.

The A solution is the reducing agent, and increasing the quantity increases the snap and body of the negative. The B solution is the preservative. Increasing it makes a grayer negative, and clears away all trace of the familiar greenish-black color of the Pyro deposit until, if enough is added, a clear gray negative is obtained which prints very quickly. By cutting down B we get more warm tone color in the deposit. The C solution controls the contrast. Using more of it will give greater contrast, and cutting down on it will give softer negatives. It also controls the speed of the developer and, if left out altogether, development will take about an hour or more.

This developer will do all that any other developer will do, and many things that no other can. Absolute control of every item is possible; contrast, color of deposit, halation. If we desire a low toned negative, soft in character, we cut down on C solution, and know that development will be slower and the values well held together. If we desire extreme contrast, as in copying a line drawing, use 1 A, 1 B, 3 C,

Bromide of Potash about ½ grain to the ounce, and about 3 ounces of water. The result will be a clear, clean, contrasty negative. Halation can be eliminated entirely by omitting to use the C solution, development taking about an hour. This is true even when using a single-coated plate and photographing directly at windows which are the sole source of light.

Many workers will object to this developer on the ground that it stains the fingers. This is not so. If the fingers are dipped in water before immersing them in the developer, frequently rinsed as development proceeds, and then afterward held in the acid hypo for a few seconds there will be no stain. If, on the other hand, the fingers should become stained, it may be removed with little trouble. A concentrated solution of Permanganate of Potash is at hand, and also a small bottle of concentrated Sulphuric Acid. These make a splendid reducer and so serve two purposes. Taking a teaspoonful of the Permanganate Solution and adding enough water until a very deep port wine colored solution results, then add eight or ten drops of Sulphuric Acid. The fingers are washed in this, become stained with the Permanganate, and are then dipped in the Hypo bath, the stain vanishing away. If trouble is experienced increase the strength of the Permanganate Solution. The acid must be used or it will not work.

PRINTING PROCESSES

A rough outline of printing processes is given

109

herein, and no more, on account of space. The actual experimenting must be done by the worker until he finds what he seems to get along best with, and then he should stick to that.

The first printing medium which every new worker will encounter is usually the familiar developing paper, so-called, really a chloride of silver paper. He will use this at first to make contact prints of his negatives to see what they are, and he is advised to stick to the soft papers always, if his hope is pictorial. Never should he use the normal or contrast papers, as they are good for anything but pictorial work. He will gradually discard these papers and use them only to proof his negatives unless he uses a printing-out paper for the purpose.

As he proceeds he will see that the chloride paper is of little use, is made cheaply with a thin emulsion, and has little possibility for the proper rendition of tone values. There are, however, high-grade chloride papers which will give good qualities, but they are never called gaslight or developing papers, all having some particular brand name. These chloride papers are used in contact printing and not for enlargement, on account of their slow speed. It is possible that they might be used for enlargement under certain circumstances where one has a very thin flat negative and a strong light, but ordinarily the exposure would be too long.

The next step is to consider the bromide and fast chloride papers for enlargement. Of all printing mediums that which is most popular with the pic-

CHORDS
R. W. Trowbridge

SAN JUAN CAPISTRANO
Fred R. Dapprich

torialist is enlargement, on account of the fact that he can use a small-sized camera and make direct prints from the negatives. It should, therefore, receive every consideration—since many never proceed beyond this point. Some of these papers are very fine and there are many kinds and brands to be obtained. With the thin negative advised for the pictorial worker the range of papers is tremendous, from the fastest bromide papers to the better grade of chloride papers. Some of the fastest bromide papers will give a flat print from the type of negative suggested even with a slow source of illumination, and in order to hold up contrast it will be necessary to use a paper which gives brilliancy. All kinds are obtainable.

The bromide paper is easily the most valuable paper for all workers, being used by most of them, and it does not require dabbling with complicated printing processes. It has the one great fault, that it curls, but has almost every other quality that one could ask of a printing paper. It is good for contact printing, giving a most exquisite scale of gradation, and, of course, is most valuable of all when used in making a direct enlargement from the small negative so popular with the pictorial worker.

The best print is obtained when the worker has to literally fight for contrast. In that way the finest gradation is obtained. Under these circumstances it is well to make a print where the exposure has to be gauged to a nicety and leave it in the developer face down until it arrives at a stopping point. Using

113

an old developer with a little fresh added as required, the best bromides are obtained, soft, full of fine gradations, and rich in tone values. A fresh developer will not make nearly so good a print.

The platinum, paladiotype, and kallitype papers all require contact printing and are too slow to be used in enlargement. If a small plate is used it will be necessary to make an enlarged negative. This negative can be made on glass or paper as the worker sees fit. The paper negative is not so good, however, as it loses the fine qualities of these superb papers on account of its grain. The glass negative is the best, and the best glass negative is that made directly in the camera. The principle of these papers lies in the fact that an iron salt is sensitive to light, and the exposure is made upon the iron salt, and not the metal which forms the image. This iron salt when placed in the developer is released and reduces the metal which forms the image. It is apparent, therefore, that since the actual exposure is made upon a salt which is not the image, and that this sensitive salt is washed away after development, definition is not as precise as in another paper wherein the sensitive metal salt is reduced. So these papers soften the quality of the definition somewhat and render a very fine quality of line. The gradation in these papers is the finest obtainable and incidentally they do not curl.

The platinotype and palladiotype papers are made commercially and can be bought, but if the worker chooses to print in kallitype he must make it. It is not so permanent, being a silver image and silver being a very fugitive metal, but the gradation is the same and it does not curl. The color, however, is not so good and is often uncontrollable.

These papers nearly all have a dead matte surface which softens the contrasts and gives a more pictorial effect. In some cases, however, it has been found that the print needed brightening and they have been waxed in order to obtain a gloss which gave better detail to the shadows. A thick floor wax is necessary as it is the only thing which will not sink into the paper, the ordinary waxing solutions not being usable. The developer combined with glycerin also gives a slight lustre which is very pleasant.

The gum print is particularly applicable to pictorial work if done well, but so many gums have been made coarse and grainy, showing brush marks, that they lost a great deal in quality. So many good manuscripts have been written about these processes, telling about them in detail, that it is best to mention them but briefly. The gum platinum is one of the refined printing processes which is recommended to the worker. Each one of these processes has virtues of its own and no one man can say that one or the other is better, so the worker must be left to do his own deciding.

Bromoil.—This is really a gelatin ink process, extremely fascinating, and one of the most popular. Whether oil or bromoil or oil transfer is used is of little moment, all being sister processes and having much the same qualities. The bromoil is the most popular, as it requires no large negative and can be made upon a bromide enlargement. The silver image is bleached out with chemicals which have a tanning effect upon the gelatin in the shadows. The print is then soaked in water until the untanned gelatin has fully swollen and absorbed water, there being no visible image when this is done. It is then inked with a stiff brush and the tones laid on as the worker sees fit, shadows deepened or lightened, as necessary, and values placed upon the print almost precisely as the worker sees fit. In fact, these are the only photographic processes where complete control of all values is possible.

They have one bad effect in that the worker has the tendency to become lazy in the selection of his pictures, knowing that he can "fix" whatever is wrong when he gets home. In other words, the picture is made more at home than in the field. The best photographic results, after all, are those in which the negative has been made perfectly. The printing can then be left for anybody to do, knowing that a good result will be obtained on any paper that will print well.

PRESENTATION

As to the presentation of the print, the various salons have come to expect a certain standard, using either a white or India tinted mount, generally not exceeding 16 x 20 inches in size and not under 14 x 17, according to the size of the print. It would seem best to stick to the larger mount for all sizes of prints, as in that case we would have a uniformity which makes the hanging of prints simpler and insures that they are not placed so close together as to interfere with individual consideration. The great trouble with exhibitions is that prints argue with each other when hung on the wall. Besides it is of great advantage to the print, when placed before a jury, to have sufficient mount to insure that nothing else intrudes upon it. That often decides a jury in favor. Presentation is very important and it is of scant use to make a fine print and then present it in such a manner that it does not appear to the best advantage. It is also a curious fact that almost any print, if well mounted and presented, will make an impression. The suggestion is made that all prints on white stock be mounted on white mounts of 16 x 20 inches, for any size to 11 x 14, and that all prints on buff stock be mounted on India mounts of the same dimensions.

With some of the materials and apparatus mentioned in this chapter it is possible to get a very fine pictorial result, with image quality so controlled as to be neither too hard or too soft, with tone values so managed by proper selection and development that the resulting negative can be printed on a chloride paper by any person with a ten minute practice. The image will not be too sharp, nor so mushy that it will destroy necessary detail; everything must be clear as to intent. The negative is exposed properly and so selected as to arrangement that tone values are right, or nearly so. The development of the negative has been carried to just the point where it will serve best, in a developer which was selected for the purpose, and adjusted to suit that picture. Then the print is a matter of routine.

CHAPTER V.

SUBJECTS

THE pictorial worker is without restriction as to subject matter so long as he does something practical with it. He can very well make a picture of an old shoe if he creates a picture with the material he selects, seeing to matters of arrangement and control of values in such a manner that the average man will be impressed, not so much with the pictures and subject matter itself, but by the way the subject is handled. This is perhaps the greatest contribution of the pictorial worker to photography. He has taken the most commonplace of material and has presented it in a manner which has excited admiration. This is, indeed, true of any of the arts, many things which in themselves are commonplace being done in a manner which is entirely different and presented in an aristocratic way. Aside from the arrangement, which in pictorial work should be a matter of great study and attention, control of tone values is one of the necessary outstanding features. Many a picture which has been cast aside as unfit for exhibition would have been quite all right if proper care had been maintained in development, printing and mounting. The study of subjects is a thing which deserves scant attention in this branch of photography, as any subject is suitable for the pictorial worker if he chooses to do it well. There are workers who could be restricted to an acre of ground, with the full knowledge that they would in that small space be able to create five hundred pictures—not find and take, but create, which is assuredly what they do.

The portrait, being of perhaps the greatest interest to the many since it concerns people and what they do, deserves the first place in any mention of pictorial subjects. It deserves first consideration also because few pictorial workers make a good portrait. It is surely pictorial, perhaps more so than any other subject which comes within the range of the camera. Each person is different from the others and deserves a separate consideration and treatment. So many things vary and have a bearing on this kind of work that it is another one of the subjects we could dismiss with the quaint observation that if we treated it fully we could not get it into the book. Many artists have spent lifetimes to master one small thing concerned with portraiture, and, while the camera is an instrument which does its drawing in a moment, it is at the same time deceitful in the respect that it lures the unsuspecting worker into thinking that as the best possible way to get a result, the proper and most desirable thing under the circumstances would be to shoot many plates and select the best afterward. This is quite an erroneous idea and seldom brings results, for careful consideration of subject is the only way to accomplish a picture which will begin to tell the character of the subject. Careful work and two plates will be

REFLECTIONS
F. M. Doudna

THE GRAY SEA
Alice Boughton

more likely to get you the real portrait than two dozen exposures carelessly shot away.

The large head is the simplest form of portrait, and is rather tricky for all since, while it does not seem to require any great thought in arrangement, it is a very curious thing that just as much placing is required as when doing a subject of many items. A fraction of an inch up or down, right or left, seems to make a great difference in the final result. The long focus lens is an essential thing, since it is obvious that using a short focus lens close to the head will not only distort but will not get nearly the full half of the head required in a portrait. While many workers use a short focus lens on the ground that it is extended greatly when focused close and really becomes a long focus lens, this does not alter the case and distortion of the head is great. It is quite necessary to have a lens which in focus equals or exceeds one and one-half times the diagonal of the plate.

The half length and full length figures lend themselves to more compositional effects, aside from character rendition which does not vary so much since we elect to use more or less of the figure. The hands are a great asset for they are spots which we have under our control as to placing, giving the worker a real control over balance. They are, however, added difficulties and each item we add, while it adds to the possibility of arrangement, naturally increases the risk of failure by adding more obstacles to stumble over. The hands likewise, while we may

123

place them where we please and gain a spot here or there as we elect, must be so handled as not to detract more than they add by their sheer awkwardness. Hands are very difficult to handle in painting and especially so in photography where they cannot be changed from what they are and the only control we have over them is to pose them in such a manner that they are at their best or to regulate their tone. We have in this item the most difficult thing in portrait photography.

The study of the full figure is not quite so difficult but the nude figure is the hurdle over which many aspiring pictorialists have their tumbles. Many workers seem to have a mania for making pictures of the nude figure and few of the pictures are ever of any use pictorially, for various reasons. The draped, or partially draped, figure is far simpler to handle and when used in a woodland setting is very interesting, in most cases being used as a white spot which is placed at the pleasure of the worker and, when used in the middle ground of the picture, is far enough from the camera not to require great effort in posing.

Group pictures very naturally follow any discussion of the single figure, or portrait, since they are composed of a number of figures. They are quite difficult to handle and seldom do we see one which is good except where the worker has absolute control in directing the figures as to location and prose. Even then he is likely to obtain nothing but failures. The haphazard shooting of groups of people by aspiring pictorialists is not a thing which can even come under discussion—it being a matter of mere chance if such pictures are successful. We are concerned only with the picture which is created and our efforts are to further that end.

In the architectural subject, wherein groups of people are used in connection with a building or portion of a building, the latter being the important subject matter of the picture, we do not consider this a picture under this class. For while we may have a subject of this kind, with groups of people strung all along the lower front to show scale and to make an important addition to the picture, even though they are properly handled the main item is architectural and the people are but incidental and thus are of second consideration.

The next subject which comes to the mind of the average worker is the all prevalent landscape. When a worker gets the idea of making a picture his thoughts turn to landscapes and naturally so, for in all literature and poetry he has read and read all about the landscape. If a writer desires to write a few more lines, he attacks the landscape because nobody can say that it is all wrong. He writes reams about the subtle lights of nature, and after dusk, and dawns, and things which are practically impossible for the camera to handle. These references are dangerous to the budding pictorialist and, while they read very well, they do not make pictorial material. They treat usually of some subtle light which cannot be photographed and not of any compositional arrangement. Few writers know anything about composition. Much has been unjustly written about nature and it has been the cause of many bad photographs. The painter too has done most of his work picturing unusual phases of nature—afterlights, dusk, weird shadows of early daylight, all matters practically impossible in photography. The worker in photography will realize from bitter experience that if he proposes to make landscapes he will finally resort to pattern composition in order to get anything which photography can handle with assurance. If he desires to play with queer dusks and dawns he will find that they are better made in the time of day when there is light to work by and then created by sound technique in the dark room. There is something in knowing the limitation of the medium, and the landscape is a subject which will show up the limitations of photography more than anything else. On the other hand, those things which are most difficult are generally the most beautiful when done properly; so the landscape has many capabilities as pictorial material.

The figure used carefully, and sparingly is a great help, since it gives a spot usually under control which many times save the picture from failure. In the foreground the figure becomes the controlling matter of the picture, so we have really a figure study with landscape setting. In painting, Gainsborough and Fragonard made many such pictures and they are worth while studying as examples of what can be done with photography.

LILLIAN GISH
© *Charles Albin*

DANCERS

Margaret DeM. Brown

The figure placed in the middle ground becomes a part of the landscape and, as such, is not the main item of the picture. Under control as to placing we have a spot which we can place as we please, which helps greatly. When the figure is well beyond the middle ground of the picture it loses power, and so has less effect upon the composition. The sum of our observations is, that the figure has the greatest value in landscape work when used in the middle ground or near middle ground for the reasons set forth above, and that it ceases to become landscape matter when used very close up and dominates the picture.

In the study of the landscape we see, if we look with any eye, that the foreground usually has a great effect upon the picture, since most formations of pattern or design are made there. In other words, the leading lines of the picture are generally controllable in the foreground. This is based upon the presumption that we are concerned with what the average person in photography understands as straight landscapes and are not making decorative designs of individual branches and trees which cannot under any circumstances be called landscape pictures. We also leave aside the typical sunset pictures, which are not pictures at all, but simply shots at the sky with enough foreground matter to hold them to earth, that is unless the sky is closely woven with the foreground and landscape items into a cohesive subject which stands as a unit, each item depending upon the other for its placing, tone and existence, the sum total making the picture. We suggest that the worker look to the foreground for the controlling items in his picture, and they will generally exist there. In fact, it is far easier to make a picture using foreground matter than by discarding it, for the foreground has far more to say than any other portion of the picture. Though the landscape is beastly when done badly, it is exquisite when done well, so have courage and try it.

Still life is perhaps one of the most controllable subjects one can attempt. Control of every item in the scale of the picture is possible, subject matter, lighting, arrangement, exposure, all. We can select what we please, place it as we please, light it as we please, and expose it as we please. It is quite simple, apparently, and yet to the average worker it is difficult, more so than other subjects. Considering every item, it is easier than any other thing to do. All we need is a few properties, vases, copper pots, oranges, apples, potatoes, earthen jugs, and still life is a lazy task. On winter days it is very comfortable to arrange various items into what we hope will be a nice picture, and then expose the plate as long or as short as we think necessary so that the tone values will be as we desire. Assuredly, still life is a pleasant subject and gives more to the worker for the effort involved than almost any other. There is no confusion of color to bother the worker; the picture is a matter of shapes and placing and comes out quite as we planned. The only obstacle in the way of the pictorialist is his ability to place the various items into a harmonious arrangement which will end up in a good composition. The long focus lens is, of course, quite a necessity.

The city offers many pictorial possibilities. Its streets, its buildings, monuments, all provide great subjects for the camera. There is no color to worry about, as the average city is a drab monotone. One is almost forced to take heed of shapes and forms alone and, when that is done, the picture is in a fair way to become real and existent. Shapes are the things which photography shows best, not color or some elusive phase of non-actinic light which will not impress itself upon the plate. A photograph well exposed is a relation of subject items which are nothing but various shapes so placed with relation to each other and to the boundaries of the picture, that harmony results. Then the picture is happy. The city almost insists upon being considered from this standpoint, and offers up exquisite conditions to the pictorial photographer. If the day is sunny there is one condition which is good; if it is foggy there is still another, that too being good, and if it rains it is again pictorially happy and in its element. No matter what the weather, the city is pictorial and is always ready for the camera regardless of season. A modern city with its tall buildings and streets like canons, is the finest of pictorial material; an ancient city, with old low buildings and the evidences of time and atmosphere of age, presents a subject that, if anything, exceeds the modern city. In any age, a city is a picture garden and the easiest kind of a spot for the pictorialist to work in.

The logical instrument is the reflex camera, one which is so made that it will allow the use of a lens of short focus. This eliminates immediately any single lens, as it is necessarily of long focus to get covering power, and, it might be added, that almost any soft focus lens is practically impossible to work with in the narrow confines of the city. Besides, it does not cover well enough where it becomes necessary to render rectilinear lines. It will be well to remember, again, that if a lens of long focus is used, which will not include the picture, the picture cannot be made, whereas if we have too wide an angle we can take plenty, and trim some off as we desire later. The latter is better than to lose pictures, as it is a simple matter to make an enlargement or an enlarged negative.

In working in and about the city, the element of human interest adds greatly to the pictorial quality. Cities are the creations of people and depend upon people for their existence. They would not be there if it were not for people who, congregating as they naturally will through some instinct that makes them desire to be near each other, built these cities. Hence, cities are basically of people, and everything about a city has something to do with people. So when we make pictures wherein the city is our subject matter, we have an intense human interest to assist us.

RICHARD BARTHELMESS
© Charles Albin

THE CLOUD
Forman Hanna

We have thousands of things to photograph which will make pictures. A quaint doorway which at a certain time of day has a fine spot of sunlight on it. We would have to time our going carefully as the spot of light is the thing which makes the picture. A watch is as much use as a camera in certain cases, since the time of making them must be precise within half an hour. We must be there just a little ahead of time, and perhaps wait until some figure gets just where we desire in order to obtain scale. Some huddled decrepit figure has more atmosphere about it, so we will wait for it to come along. The picture must be good or the time has been wasted. This is but one little item in the thousands of others which one can find for the camera. Perhaps some well-known street, so taken that we create a new thought about it that was not apparent before, or some place which is so presented that people could see that a new angle is considered. Some narrow canon of street with many little figures at the bottom of the picture which give it tremendous scale. All are good pictorial material.

The waterfront and the docks make a fairyland for the pictorialist. Where the ships come in from the sea, and picturesque slouching seamen spot them-selves into position here and there against the outline of ships. Beyond are the shapes and lines of the city. The waterfront has many sides, and the camera is very happy in such a place.

Each person has had some particular experience with subjects of such a nature that he is inclined

135

to remember all other subjects by these experiences, perhaps ones of which he has some knowledge. One has only his own experience to go by. For instance, the waterfront of many cities varies considerably, from the quaint docks of some oriental city to the waterfront of New York, backed up against high spires of buildings. There is all the difference imaginable. And yet these same waterfronts have many characteristics which are identical and which have the same general effect in the picture. The sea has placed its stamp upon them and, while the forms may be different, the longshoreman of the Atlantic Coast is much the same in viewpoint as the coolie who loads a junk. The things which make a picture are not always the forms, although they have a lot to do with it. So when the waterfront is touched upon, it is not with any idea of location, and yet location will creep into one's description regardless of any attempt to maintain impartiality in pictorial application. The waterfront of New York, for instance, is quite the most fascinating place that the writer has ever been with a camera. It has a million and one possibilities and, if one were to be confined to any special location, what could be more of a pictorialist's paradise than just such a place? It has everything for the picture-maker—men, ships, docks, little watery byways full of queer reflections, many patterns of odd sorts, in all an endless set of items which make an infinite number of things to photograph. It changes every day as ships come and go, and the same spot is different each time you go there. It has an atmosphere, and there is little difference whether you are there on a dull or clear day or one which is foggy. It is all so many-sided and interesting that any picture-maker could spend a lifetime there, happy with the thought that he has a subject which is perhaps the best of all. Curiously enough, this same thing may be said of any subject you really become acquainted with. The sea, the landscape, the still life, any subject, has just the same appeal when one really gets to know it.

Many workers have become well-known for their photographs of marines and spend their spare time doing just that. Whether it is a coast where the sea boils against the rocks, or long, low, sandy reaches, pictures are there just the same. Ships come into the pictures, and the worker has again a fine set of items to weave into compositions. The nature of this subject is one which almost insists upon being taken on a horizontal or landscape picture space, since the essential lines are level and long. But it does not follow that a vertical picture is not quite as good if used properly. The marshes, the sandy shores, the ships, the sea, the dunes are all very pictorial items. The reflex naturally is the most usable camera for this kind of work, although it does not follow that any camera is not good. Some of the illustrations have been selected especially to show what can be done with apparently simple material, provided the worker has the heart for his task. Once again pictures are made, not taken.

The architectural subject is perhaps one of the most interesting in pictorial photography, provided one will take the trouble to learn something about architecture. This is an essential, and many workers, well-known pictorially, have made some very ludicrous architectural studies through their ignorance of architecture. In fact, the writer has seen but few good architectural photographhs made by persons who call themselves pictorial workers, all because they know nothing about the subject which they are trying to picture. They will insist upon doing such absurd things as to make a picture of a doorway of poor design, showing that, if they did know the subject, they are certainly deficient in taste. If they took the trouble to take some primer of architecture, of which there are many, they could, in a few evenings, get themselves in better shape to do such work and make far more intelligent pictures. Architecture is perhaps the grandest of the arts and controls so many others— music, painting, sculpture, decoration that it deserves better treatment from the photographer.

It is, incidentally, the only true history of our human existence and tells the story of man as no writer ever could see it, truthfully, without prejudice, for all to read as they can. It carries a story of human ventures and activities which no other subject can ever have and deserves the best of treatment from the picture-maker. It is, besides, more difficult to pictorialize than any other subject, being more uncontrollable and requiring closer study. It has rigid lines which require careful handling and perfect placing on the plate. The lens must be rectilinear. No soft focus lens will do the work. In fact, no long focus lens will do at all, a lens well corrected and of great covering power being necessary. The pictures will, under these conditions, have to be taken sharp and if diffusion is possible it must be done afterward. Much diffusion is not good, as the detail in architecture, so carefully worked out, is quite necessary and if photographed properly must be kept as part of the picture.

Architecturally, America is woefully weak as compared with Europe and England, the latter having a long and romantic history which is practically all represented in its structures. Many fine buildings have been erected and time has added its veneer of beauty to their original fineness of design. As the buildings become older, they invariably improve in charm and become better subjects for the camera.

As mentioned, a short focus lens of good covering power is required. It is better to have several lenses of various focal length in order that, no matter how the subject presents itself, it can be so composed as to cover the plate. The fact that many rigid lines present themselves, makes the tripod almost necessary, as it is difficult to place them on the plate perfectly without convergence or slant unless a stand is used. The so-called convertible lens is of no use in this work when used singly, as the lines come out curved.

These subjects are ventured, without order or reason, as possible ideas for the adventurer into pictorial realms. They are just suggestions, and there are doubtless many things left out which ought to be included and quite a number of things mentioned which might as well be left out. It is a haphazard chapter, touching lightly here and there on pictorial subjects. It is really very pleasant to wander mentally over various things which are interesting and provide moments of pleasure. This is one thing which we may hope to gain from our venture into pictorial subjects.

CHAPTER VI.

MAKING THE PICTURE

IN setting out to make a photograph, it is essential that the worker, in order to insure its power to live, shall premeditate what he is about to do, and not haphazardly photograph that which presents itself. A picture must be created and, in order that it shall be created, the photographer must plan it out. Then, if well composed and thought out, it is a real work.

Of course there are subjects wherein one is more or less forced to work at random. If the worker proposes to walk along the waterfront and take his chance as to what he may find in the way of pictorial material, he is really gambling his time against the chance of finding subject matter. But when he does find material that pleases him he must set about planning the picture, and each time it must be so planned in order to stand as a real picture. This business of walking out, camera in hand, is a favorite one of the pictorial worker and nothing can be said against it. If he desires to do it, it is his own affair. Curiously enough, good pictures seldom result from this procedure and the photographer generally comes home tired and unhappy, more or less dissatisfied with the waste of effort. Another time he may come to a subject which at a certain time of day gives a picture he is delighted with. He thinks about it, builds it into various lines and masses, mentally, and dwells upon it day after day until he cannot rest until he makes that picture. Then one fine day when conditions are right, as he supposes, he takes the camera to that spot all prepared to really make the picture, and in this instance he has planned it. It has been in his mind a long time and he knows what he desires to do with it. He has planned long and, we hope, well. He makes several different exposures of it, variously timed in order to get the tone relation as he desires, and of slightly varying arrangements so that perhaps one of them will come out as a salon picture. This time the picture is getting fair treatment. It is being schemed just as an architect would work out a design, and from it generally comes a good result.

We are then forced to accept the idea that when one proposes to make a picture, a real picture, whether by photography or other means, it is necessary to study or plan it in such a manner that it will in some way express the intention of the creator, and that it shall fully advise the person who looks at it what was the intention of the person who created it. If it fails in expressing its intent, then the artist has failed to make himself clear and the picture is not a perfect expression. It is ambiguous.

In photography this requires a perfect command of technique. The mechanisms must be left aside, so fully at command that they are intuitively in use all the time. The good workman does not have to think of how to use his tools. And so in any branch,

142

CLARE EAMES
© *Charles Albin*

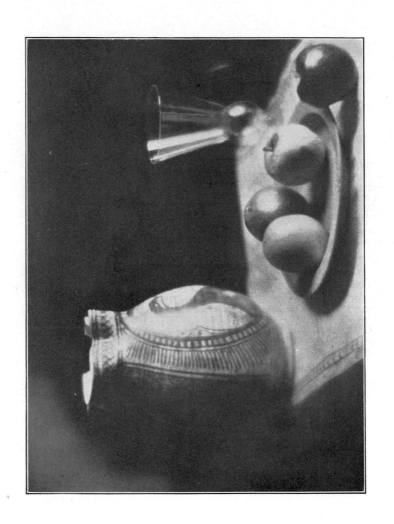

STILL LIFE
Clara E. Sipprell

painting, sculpture, as well as photography, technique is necessarily intuitive from long use, so that the full thought may be used in rendering the subject, truthfully, and with atmosphere. By atmosphere we do not mean mist as the casual photographic worker might assume and, in fact, most do. Atmosphere, as mentioned here, means that the real feeling of the subject has been captured and brought to view in a subtle manner, and that there is something in the picture which cannot be expressed in terms of line and mass. It is most aptly described as "feeling."

LIGHTINGS

The study of lightings is quite necessary, since light is the substance which actually does the work of making the image of the photograph and, for that reason alone, is the most important thing in all photography. Necessarily a study of the character of light and its power and manner of working, is a requirement which is first to be considered.

In planning the picture, if the worker depends upon nature's light, he must be fully acquainted with the orientation of his subject so that he will know when the lighting is at its best. Lighting has a great effect, and a variation of angle or intensity will sometimes make the difference between good and bad.

The motion picture has done much to bring to the attention of the photographic world the values of various lightings and their effect upon the picture. While their application is theatrical, all the work usually being controlled by directors from the theatre world whose understanding of lightings is dramatic rather than pictorial, the effect is quite the same. The mere fact that so many thousands of dollars are expended upon a picture and that the possible earnings depend to a certain extent upon its quality, has made them try almost everything possible in seeking for effects which have a value from the box office standpoint. It is a fact that nothing makes men try so hard as the prospect of some reward at the end of their labors and, as we profit by their efforts, the result is good after all. So while long-haired artists rant about man's commercial strivings and decry his efforts in that direction, good comes of it, especially in cases like this. The money lure makes them try, and the photographic world really learns about lightings.

In recent times artificial lightings have occupied a prominent position in photography, since the worker is supposed to be freed from vagaries of weather and lack of light due to cloudy days and time of year. This is true mostly of indoor work, although motion picture companies now use powerful arc lamps outdoors to relieve shadow detail even on sunny days, taking along a small power plant for their electric current.

The writer feels that while artificial light has great uses and eases the burden of the photographer who sometimes has to have it for the production of pictures upon which there is a time limit, it has made the pictorialist forget the soft beauty of natural

146

light. It has been altogether too easy to turn on a twin arc on a dull day. It was so easy that it blinded the photographer to the fact that he was sacrificing quality for comfort. Let the worker try some negatives in a good north light and then make some by any artificial light, comparing the results. No argument is required to force an understanding of the facts. The natural light is better. Rembrandt had no arc lamps to work by and where is the photograph to excel his hand work?

There is space for a brief touch upon the possibilities of lightings. We can cover but few of the many items which should be discussed fully, perhaps enough to get the worker started in some direction where he will explore further for himself. This is, after all, the greatest thing that can happen as only in original investigation can any person uncover information which is of use to him. It is simple to tread the paths made by others and, while one is bound to learn something no matter where he goes, that which he gets by himself is better than all the rest.

Under these circumstances, no matter what statements we make, we can be of little help unless the photographer will take up the trail and venture further into a kingdom which is all his own. In that he will establish the individuality which will make him heard from in later years. In order to accomplish anything, a man has to establish his identity, so that his work will be known as different from that of all others and so that people will desire

147

to see it. Then he is a cog in the human machine which cannot be replaced. When he gets to this point in photography, he becomes one of the Whites, Stieglitz or Steichens of the craft and he will not be forgotten.

To return to lightings. In the first place, "over-lighting" in motion picture parlance is perhaps as bad as "under-lighting." Not that it does any actual harm so far as exposure is concerned but, when an unusual amount of light is introduced into any room, the result is a spraying of light to such an extent that there is no control of shadow. And after all, the greatest value of light and its control is but to be able to regulate the shadows.

Suppose we take an arc lamp of high intensity in a room of about twenty feet square. The modern heavy arc lamp which has carbons one inch in thickness is the kind we have in mind, and it gives a tremendous candle power. Suppose we use two of these lamps and place them behind a screen. The room has a medium light wall surface and is so severely "overlighted" that a snapshot can be made with the lens stopped to f 11. The light has so permeated every portion of the room and has reached such a degree of diffusion, on account of the quantity, that a flat lighting results. There is plenty of light, too much, but it is not of the proper quality because it is of too great a quantity. The result is worse than no light.

The quantity of the light has some effect, therefore, upon the quality. We must determine, when using

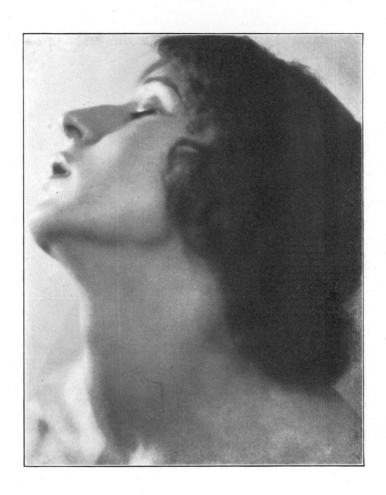

"DESHA"
Nickolas Muray

HUBERT STOWITTS—DANCER
Nickolas Muray

artificial light, what quantity we desire and work to that amount and see if we cannot control it in a manner which will give the negative we wish. It has always been the opinion of the writer that artificial light is far more difficult to understand and control than natural light. But after all, the purpose is to make a negative of a certain quality, and the light which does it best is the one for the photographer to use. Commercial requirements demand artificial light in most cases in order that a necessity can be met and we cannot, therefore, set it aside from mere preference. We must do the best we can with it.

The types of lighting are manifold and to know a few of them well is better than to have a nodding acquaintance with many. One must know and understand them in such a manner that they are under command when needed, and they must be so infused into his technique that they are really useful. It is just as essential that the photographer understand the character of light as to know the emulsion on his plate and what it will do. Light is as much a material of the photographer as silver bromide. It is the engraving tool which cuts the picture into the sensitive emulsion on the plate, so we study it as a material in photography. As discussed scientifically, light is a wonderful substance of an essential body and relating to other forces of nature. It is fair to venture the thought that perhaps it does add something to the emulsion to affect it as it does.

In the study of light, perhaps the best subject would be one spherical in shape. An orange will do

151

very well but perhaps it might be better to use something a little larger, say a child's toy balloon blown up to a diameter of about eight inches, or any spherical object about that size and light in color. That will be large enough to show easily the effect of light at a moderate distance. Then we will select an incandescent light on a cord, so that we may move it around and about the object in such a manner that we may at pleasure illuminate it from any direction. We will also have a white cardboard about twenty-four inches in diameter. These are the tools with which we will study simple lightings.

Setting the balloon upon a table we will first light it from directly in front, and on a level, and watch the effects of the light upon it from a distance of about four feet. Notice that, while the lighting is a so-called flat lighting, the center of the sphere is brighter than the edges and that we have an effect of curvature of the balloon in spite of the fact that the light is flat. We then move the light nearer the sphere and note that the illumination of the center, or portion nearest the light, gets brighter much more than the sides as we may call them, showing that if the source of light is brought closer an increase in contrast is obtained. We see also that the sides receive less light, as the light gets closer and strikes them at a more acute angle, and that the sphere is not illuminated over half its area. Now move the light away, and it will be noted that more of the area receives the light, and that while less in intensity is of a more even quality than before. Light

152

intensity is as the square of the distance. The distances of the portion nearest the light and of that away from it are more nearly identical to each other, thus cutting down the contrast of the lighting of the sphere.

We will now raise the light up vertically, keeping it still directly in front of the sphere. The upper portion will now be lighted and the under part in shadow. We could use the human head as a study, and it might be better, but we believe that the experiment on some object will give a quick study of all the lightings possible with a single source of illumination and that it will illustrate the principles better. The entire experiment can be made in less time than it takes to read this portion and will be an easy, quick study to the most experienced worker. It is curious what we have missed among the simple things and an electric light upon a flexible cord will tell us far more than we could learn in a week of reading. To make photographs with such a light, thinking that the understanding of lightings will come as a result, is not good. The only way to know light is to study light, without anything else to bother. Many principles will be visible and once digested will never be forgotten. They can then be applied to any case which one may meet.

Now move the light to the left and to the right, nearer and then further away, higher and lower, noting carefully the effect in each case. Then bring the white cardboard into position to reflect light upon the dark side of the sphere, moving it about at

153

various heights, angles and positions until its effect is noted from every position. The shadow is relieved and, no matter how short the exposure, under these circumstances there could be no clear glass in the negative.

Suppose then we take another object, any cubical thing. Put it through the same series of lightings. Use the reflector, moving the light nearer and further away, and watch every effect. Now bring the camera into play. Make an exposure of every position of lighting without the reflector and with it, and make proofs.

Now suppose we take a flat surface, the cardboard itself. A simple demonstration is possible, of the fact that bringing the light closer will increase the contrast. Place the light far away from the card and it is evenly illuminated all over the surface. Bring it right against the surface, at the center, and note that while the card is brilliantly illuminated at the center portion, the edges are receiving but little light and that at an angle. This proves the point. From the foregoing we then arrive at some opinions regarding the effect of light upon a sphere, a cube and a flat surface. From this we can very nearly know what effect it has upon any object.

Suppose we now consider a subject which we would make a picture of. A person is more susceptible to the character of the light than anything else, so we use one as our subject. First the flat lighting. What does it do? Firstly it eliminates nearly all modeling in the face, and it follows that all wrinkles

"STUDY IN SHADOW"
Mercedes Desmore

HUBERT STOWITTS—DANCER
Nickolas Muray

and lines must be lessened by such lighting. So if we desire to make the old younger and eliminate lines, and character incidentally, we will use the flat light.

We will now move the light higher, still keeping it in front of the sitter; nearly all the lines return again. The eye sockets become dark and the whole effect is more of a character, but perhaps not so pleasant; more ghoulish, so to speak. So if we desire a dramatic effect we can use a top lighting. It will preserve all the character lines and accent certain things. This is not only true of top lightings but of any lightings that are away from the dead flat position, either right or left. The concentration of the light has also an effect upon this item. If we concentrate it in a spot, it is theatrical; dramatic somewhat, but mainly theatrical. We can continue to move the light here and there upon the human model and in that way arrive at a great many conclusions, each for himself, and usable as such for the man who makes the experiment.

In the human face lines are increased, and also the rendering of character, as we move the light away from the center or flat position either vertically or horizontally. If we have a person with a very rough seamed face which we hope to relieve a little, we adopt the flat light; if we have a smooth face which we would add character to, we adopt a more severe lighting.

Aside from the modeling or conformation of the face, the lines have a most important effect and we can deal with them almost as we please by modifying

157

the light. There seems, however, to be one form of lighting which does for almost all cases and types, and that is the familiar forty-five degree lighting wherein the light is forty-five degrees from the position of directly in front and forty-five degrees up from the horizontal. It may be that we have arrived at this conclusion by association, as it is a characteristic of man that he considers that thing best which he knows well, but counting all things, it seems to have something that other lights do not. It has many advocates—artists, architects, others—and there is reason to say that it answers all purposes best. Used indoors with some form of relief for the shadow side, it makes a perfect lighting for portraiture. For architectural subjects it is by far the best lighting.

We turn to the consideration of the back lightings, the eccentric lightings as it were, wherein the light is in any position beyond the subject and working against the camera. We also include in those lightings that which is at right angles. In this we cannot include the light from the sunset or dying day, as it is a normal light. It does not come under any consideration of lightings we may make, since at such times it is really a flat light with no foreground object accented.

It is more or less unnatural to use any light except that which is somewhere behind the camera, which after all, gives one a range of 180 degrees. One sees with difficulty against any light, and so does the camera. Detail is buried in shadows, and it is difficult to make a photograph which will give anything like a true rendering of the values visible. In fact, the values are not really visible to any instrument, even the eye, but are so only as the eye sweeps across the scene and registers the various items of light values to the mind, which is more elastic. In any form of back lighting outdoors, we find an atmospheric haze which must be carefully taken care of, else the whole impression will be lost. These lightings seem to be normal in nature, more than in portraiture, or in work where there are figures. In movies they are simply trick lightings used for effect, to dazzle the audience. In such cases they are scarcely legitimate lightings, made for the purpose of getting better pictorial results, but are circus-like antics made to lure nickels into the house. Motion picture people seldom understand what a picture is, and their work has degenerated into a form of photographic trickery which cannot exist very much longer as it is, since it is so absurd and is done by persons who know little about the better side of photography. The business is growing into a large industry and is in the hands of ex-furriers and vaudeville men, who will soon pass on to give way to those who really can add something to the work.

In calling the back and side lightings eccentric, we do so for the reason that the photographer who uses them, takes advantage of a certain sensational element in human nature and, while these lightings are not good, they are flashy and take the average eye. The picture gets by as artistic, while it is precisely otherwise. The photographer gains

159

a few dollars, but it is a poor way to get them. How absurd are these spotty, back-lighted things alongside the dignified and permanent pictures made by more conventional means! They will be despised and cast aside in a few years. If the photographer has any form of composition or pattern in his picture, he need indulge in no trick lightings to gain a standard. We find them invariably used where there are compositional defects and the picture needs some form of dressing up in order that it shall not pass by unnoticed. In this case it is noticed, as a gaudy billboard would be noticed, to be praised only by those who do not know.

Even so we cannot say that side lightings are to be condemned altogether, as there may be cases where they are entirely legitimate. Usually they are "fakes," so to speak, and the greatest instance is the typical movie back lighting.

There are cases in landscape photography where the light is of such an indeterminate direction that it is practically impossible to see from which direction it comes. It is not so prominent as in other subjects but, of course, it must not be neglected. If one will take the trouble to look at many landscape paintings, he will note that in over half the cases the lighting is entirely flat, or that the subject is one where there is a mist, or perhaps a dusk scene. Painters seldom wish to be hampered by curious lightings, and assuredly they have made a more comprehensive study of the landscape than photographers. We do not wish to indicate that the photographer shall follow the path of the painter in any case, as some unfortunately do for, in so doing, they are losing the contact with the photographic medium and its greatest values are destroyed. The idea is merely presented that the painter has studied lightings and that we can take advantage of his research, rather than to begin all over again.

PERSPECTIVE

Perspective is a most mathematical matter. We hear various things about it, about long focus and short focus lenses, and very few clear statements as to what it is, and what affects it. If the worker will turn to the architect he will perhaps learn more about it than he can from any other person.

The focus of the lens has nothing to do with perspective, contrary to general opinion. It is altogether a matter of point of view. If we stand off from a subject we get gentle and less angular lines, no matter what lens we use. Only the size of the image is affected. If we take a picture of a building or object with two different lenses from the same distance, the lines of perspective are the same. And if we enlarge the picture made with the short focus lens until the image is the same size as that made with the long focus lens, the lines will all have the same angles and the perspective will be identical. The wide angle lens takes in more, and thus it appears that the lines are more angular and the perspective different, but this is not so, and perspective is only changed by the position of the camera.

161

If we consider any object, say a sphere, we will note many things which will assist us in the study of perspective. Taking a position ten feet away from a ball of eight inches diameter, note that we can see just so far around it. If we increase that distance we can see further around the sphere, and if we go far enough away from it we can see the full half, that distance being in reality infinity, but for practical purposes we will say that infinity is a hundred feet. Then at one hundred feet we can see half way around the sphere, or 180 degrees of its surface. Let us approach it and we will note that we see less and less as we do so. We can come so close that we see but 90 degrees of its surface, or one-quarter. We can take a position upon the surface of the sphere, and let us suppose we are very small and that the sphere is much larger than we are. We find that we cannot see any appreciable portion of the surface of the sphere, perhaps but one degree, and have a case analogous with our own position upon the earth. We can apply this same experiment to the human head, and immediately see that it is wise to keep far from it in order that we can show the full half of it in the picture. We use a long focus lens under these circumstances, not to get "better perspective" but to get a large head upon the plate. The perspective depends upon the distance from the head, and only upon that. By moving far enough away from any object we gain more of a view of it much as we see the moon or the sun.

When we think of perspective we can only bring

the lens into play after we have digested the subject as to line and angle. The lens is used only to make the image size as we desire it. Perspective is not the victim of the lens in any respect, except that one moves up to get a larger image, and a change in perspective results. But we must learn to disassociate the two in order that we may understand each one fully. In properly making a picture we study the subject and decide upon the position from which we are going to photograph it, thinking at the time only of how the lines look to us in perspective. Once that is done, we set up the camera and see how big the image is going to be and select the lens which will make it of the size we desire. We have covered two entirely different ideas in doing this. In order to do this we would require a battery of lenses of different foci, and in truth the worker should have them, but since that is sometimes impracticable we take the picture smaller and enlarge it when we get home. We do not move up to get the image larger, as we would then sacrifice the most important item, perspective. When we enlarge the small image we have the same result as if we had taken the picture with a long focus lens.

By drawing it is possible to derive two meanings. One the angular perspective of the picture itself, and the other the character of the line used, sharp or diffused. They depend upon each other to a certain extent, and we shall consider their relation.

First of all, the human eye sees an angle of about two degrees, which is very small. The image is impressed upon a focal plane, or retina, which closely resembles the inside of a sphere. It is not flat like a plate. The angle of vision is so small, however, that the picture to all intents and purposes is impressed upon a flat plane, or one very nearly so, on account of the small portion of the spherical surface used for receiving the image. Still it is not flat and, as such, cannot be compared with the photographic plate in any sense, other than the angle of vision included and the point of view as related to the camera.

Since the eye sees but a very small angle it has to visualize any object by sweeping across it in all directions. It cannot take it all in at one glance. The eye is the instrument of the mind, rather than a purely mathematical instrument like the lens of photography, and it is difficult to compare them in any sense. But when the eye sees, it actually sees but a very small angle, and half sees beyond a certain area, the half-seen portion being comprehended by the mind, as it happens. The fact is that the mind sees rather than the eye, for the eye sees upside down, and the mind so controls the vision that all objects appear right side up. It is also true that the eye sees only what the mind knows about and that it cannot see what the mind does not understand, proving that it is altogether an instrument of the mind and in no way comparable with a lens. It also has an automatic diaphragm control which lets in just as much light as the retina is capable of taking care of properly, while the lens has not. It is possible to

A DOORWAY
Dr. A. D. Chaffee

SHADOW

Dr. D. J. Ruzicka

make a photographic objective which will have such
an automatic diaphragm control, but not very simple
and it would have to be adjusted for every different
plate. This has been done in a way for engravers on
account of their difficulties—stop values being affectd
by the various extensions of the camera.

According to most photographic critics, the main
thing which affects the subject of eye and lens is
the angle of vision. They have stated time and
again that if we had a lens which most closely ap-
proached the angle of the eye we would get better
perspective. The comparison will not hold water
and the writer disputes it totally. Many fine pictures
have been made at angles of nearly one hundred
degrees whereas the eye sees but two degrees
properly. A picture is simply a relation of items of
subject matter so placed upon a rectangular space
as to present a certain thought, or emotion, whereas
the eye makes no attempt to do that. The eye simply
sees, and sees so much, and the mind comprehends
what it sees. If the mind after that proposes to take
the items in the vision of the eye and place them
on a rectangular space, it has nothing to do with
the eye at all. We can compare the eye with the
photographic lens, discuss it, and think about it, all
in the hope that we may arrive at something which
will assist us in making a picture. But the comparison is unjust and unmeaning, and the making of
a picture is a mental proceeding while the vision
of the eye is a purely mechanical thing directed by
the brain of the man.

Suppose we consider the hand at arm's length, with fingers outstretched. Look intently at one finger of the hand. It will be noticed that while one sees that finger clearly, the other fingers are not seen clearly, but are realized, as to size and location. We know that they are there, and that helps us to see them dimly. If we desire to see one of the other fingers clearly we have to shift the gaze, and in order to see the five fingers we have to look at each one of them. We see them all, one after the other so quickly that we do not realize that we see them one at a time. The mind holds each finger in place while the eye sweeps across them, so that finally the whole hand is "seen," as it were, but it is seen by the mind. If we visualize a wide angle as it happens, the eye sweeps across the various items and the mind fixes them in place until we see the whole, but never clearly at one time, except in the mind. Close the eyes after doing this experiment, and the subject is seen more clearly than if the eyes were held open. The mind relates the several items, and fixes them into a composition, if a picture is contemplated.

Suppose then we decide to place such a series of items upon a photographic plate. We are going to make a picture. It may be a wide angle subject and it may not. It does not matter. The mind covers a very wide angle, wider than any lens. We might philosophize about the angle being too great and that it cannot be a picture. We have heard as much among so-called pictorialists, but we can do as we please so long as we make a picture, wide angle and all. Once the picture is made, we make a print, and then we see it all at one look as it were, by standing away from it. The eye at last sees the subject all in one glance, and is happy. And what makes the picture is any set of items which will so occur on the picture space that they will please the mind, not the eye. The eye is but a telegraph instrument.

What has an effect is the size of the print. If it is too big we have to back off to see it all at once, as we should. There is a limit to size. On the print it should be visible all at once. An 8 x 10 held at arm's length is seen well, and an 11 x 14 has to be seen further away. Here we have angle in the picture itself, and in this case it is well to make it of a size that will be seeable at once at a moderate distance, so that the eye may not have to send the message to the brain piecemeal, one item after the other.

If all the foregoing is true, and we believe it is, we then reach the conclusion that any lens will do, any angle or any focus, so long as we put a picture upon the print for the eye to look at. On the other hand, the angle of the lens has quite an effect pictorially, but not as compared with the angle of vision of the eye. While we are at liberty to use any lens we desire, there are certain objections to this, from the pictorial standpoint, since with wide angle lenses we add more items to the view. The picture is likely to become complicated, and the business of choosing a good arrangement from so many items is difficult. The worker has a simpler task if he

169

chooses to use a small angle and work together those items which he includes in such a manner that they will relate well. It is all comparative, and nothing real can be stated. The most perfect tool to work with is assuredly the wide angle lens, for with it anything which confronts the worker can be photographed and included in the picture. Then if he should happen to make a picture wherein he has his composition all on one small portion of the plate, he can enlarge that portion. On the other hand, this is quite the most difficult method of working, with many technical disadvantages, and has the extreme difficulty of composing the picture without the assistance of the edges. The mind is taxed greatly and there are few workers who can do this and get anything worth while. We are reluctantly forced to decide that the best method, pictorially, is to use a lens which includes an angle of about 30 degrees, which gives a lens of focal length equal to about twice the long side of the plate.

DRAWING

By drawing in this case we mean the type of line used in making the picture, whether diffused or sharp.

Pictorialists have of late years accepted the soft focus lens without cavil, after a long feud as to which was best, fuzzy or sharp. They turn one way and then the other, and we see the majority prefer fuzzy, and then in ten years sharp images. It does not matter much, so long as they are happy and make

STILL LIFE
Arthur Hammond

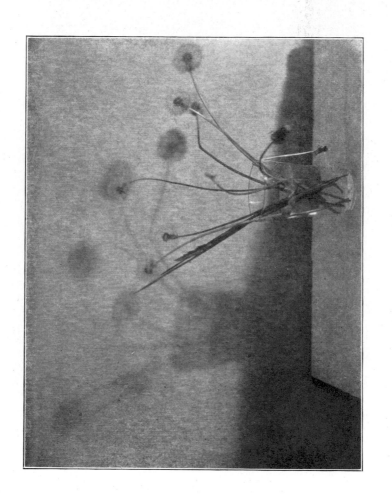

"STILL LIFE"
Adele C. Shreve

good pictures. The pictures are pleasant, if they are happy in composition and technique. They are then past the little people who make them, and will last a longer time than the photographers. We choose diffusion as we please, or sharp, but if we remember to make good compositions, sharp or fuzzy, it does not matter.

Diffusion has its virtues, and is likable in place. It has been a nightmare in many cases when used indiscriminately by the average worker who thinks that fuzz means pictorial value. That we must not do. Diffusion, however, has been generally accepted, despite this handicap. Years ago it was accepted for the first time, curiously enough about the time the modern anastigmat became a real lens. Once lenses were made so perfect that they would make wiry, sharp lines, it became necessary to make lenses which would not do so. The wiry lines were so insistent that they hurt the pictures. They were hard, as to image. They were so hard that they could not be softened easily, and so we have the soft focus lens. At first workers used old lenses which were poorly corrected, but they were not right. A lens for the purpose was demanded. The old lenses made soft pictures because they were badly corrected and could not do otherwise. The new soft focus lenses made soft pictures, of a quality, because they were designed to do so. It is better. From that point on we have the division, soft or sharp.

The only trouble with the advent of the soft focus lens was that it got into the hands of people who did

173

not realize that it should be used to make a picture with, and who fuzzed everything they saw. They could point the camera out the back door with the idea that pictures were now automatic. Fuzz made a picture. This was the thing which brought the pictorial world to its senses, and very quickly. They soon realized that if photography was not to be a toy for all to play with, they had better get seriously to work making pictures which do not depend upon definition of any sort for their qualities. This is what happened.

This does not alter the case that the character of the line, as softened or sharp, has an effect upon the picture, and that we should know about it. We have passed the fanatical stage where fuzz makes a picture, and now set ourselves to the study of diffusion and to learn how we may use it, little or much, so that we will improve the pictures. We use it or not, as we desire, to accomplish something. The question arises as to just what is the right amount to use in a pictorial photograph. That will never be answered. It is the same amount as the sugar you use in your coffee, and each person has a different idea and they are all right. We can discuss it and see if we can throw some light upon it, but that is all.

If we set an amount of diffusion for the worker to use, we would only eliminate all individuality and standardize pictures. Photography is not engineering, where formulæ are known and methods established for nearly all conditions. Even in engineering there is plenty of room for individual thought, as against standardization, and we find innovations even there in advance of the science, which are accepted as standards as they become known. In the same respect pictures are accepted as good and imitated, become standardized in a sense, and we see many photographs in which we can trace the inspiration which prompted the "manufacturer" to make them. "Manufacturer" is the proper word in this case.

In order to establish some designation for diffusion, let us say that extreme diffusion is that which might be the limit of use without losing the actual massing of the items in the picture. In other words, it is the extreme point to which diffusion can be carried without losing the picture altogether. There is no detail whatever, in the smaller items in the picture, and only the main masses hold their identity. We do not comment upon whether this is good or bad, only to designate it as the extreme. It so happens that it is good taste in some cases and bad in others, and it is described so that we will have something to go upon.

From the degree of diffusion just described to full sharp, there are many modulations of softness, which have many uses. The sharp picture has its use and as mentioned, the definition is not so much the point in question as the effect; and dead sharp when well handled with soft development and printing is one way to make a picture without wiry quality. But it is very difficult to handle technically, and the aver-

175

age worker is unable to do it, under which circumstances we will say that sharp pictures are not so good, and had better be left aside as pictorially impossible. The hard line is difficult to handle pictorially. Something between dead sharp and extremely diffused is what we would select, with no clear idea as to just what until the subject is selected. Of course, the mushy, foggy type of picture, wherein the halo of the soft focus lens is allowed to creep all over is not to be considered in any case. Extreme halo or double line is as bad, and good photography has no place for it.

In the selection of diffusion we must consider subject matter, its distance from the camera, and the character of the subject. In the case of large heads we can use all the diffusion possible, since the items are large and we can do so without losing character. The skin texture will be rendered smoother. On the other hand, many fine pictures are made with the lens used sharp but, as said, this is difficult. In photographing the half and full length figure, we are forced to use less diffusion, since the detail becomes smaller as the subject is moved further away from the camera and, being so, cannot stand as much diffusion without losing character. Detail must be held, but can be subdued. The very word detail tells us about its value in the picture, and that it must be held back in its proper place as such, as detail, not to assume too great a value. So we find that the details of the subject become smaller as we recede from it, and that we must use less diffusion

STILL LIFE
A. P. Milne

PACK TRAIN
Forman Hanna

or we will lose it entirely. This is also true in other subjects, landscape, still life, marines, architecture, and all work where the essential detail exists smaller in the picture.

With the average soft focus lens it is necessary to stop down in order to get firmer drawing, and in so doing one loses speed. This is an advantage in some cases where depth is required, but a disadvantage in others. There are lenses in which the diffusion does not depend upon the diaphragm, and they are more useful in all work.

As a contradiction to the foregoing, there are cases where the absolute elimination of detail is effective, particularly where large masses are predominant in the picture. Based upon the knowledge that the fewer the tones the better is the probability of getting a simplicity of rendering, we can by the intelligent use of extreme diffusion destroy all detail until the main masses are rendered in perfect simplicity without anything to distract, and only the tone values of those masses will appear. It is a very interesting method of pictorializing and effective as well as good, and we usually find in a picture done in this manner but two or three tones and those well valued. Of course, this treatment requires fine handling and good arrangement, or it will fall down as a picture. There is no lens made which will give the extreme of diffusion required and it will have to be obtained by taking the negative first with a diffused focus lens, used with all possible softness and no halo, and a print made with still more diffusion. Great care

179

must be taken to see that the familiar wooliness does not occur as that is impossible. Perhaps the simplest way to do this is to work in a small size, using a portion of the negative and then enlarging it again with the soft focus lens. Enlargement with the soft focus lens, while impossible from the wiry, sharp negative, gives quite a good result when done directly from the soft focus negative.

FIGURE STUDY
Francis Bruguiere

THE MARSH
Edith R. Wilson

CHAPTER VII.

COMPOSITION

THIS is the most important item in photography, or in any other kind of picture making. It is not what you have to say, but how you say it. The subject matter in photography is, to a certain extent, what you say and you have not so much control over it; but one has control over how he makes the picture of that subject matter, how it is spaced, and how he chooses to render it into tone values. That is how he says it, and it is easily the paramount item in all pictorial photography.

While we can say that technique is quite another part of photography, we must admit that the selection of tone values and their position in the picture is really a part of composition, and in the same breath we have to admit that this control of values is altogether technical for, if we place them ever so carefully and minutely, the fact remains that if we lose the values and make them too heavy or too light, we lose their compositional value in the picture. So we face the fact that composition, insomuch as the execution of it is concerned, depends upon the technical skill of the worker, and that his technique must be such that he knows what he can do with each item of the picture as to tone and line drawing. Unless this is done fully, all his efforts at spacing and placing will go for nothing. Composition and technique are dependent upon each other, and either one alone has

183

no value, so in commenting upon the former we have to consider the latter at every step. In that way technique is a matter that has to be worked out fully and carefully, and while doing this the worker can make his study of composition.

The third important item in the picture is feeling. Almost impossible to describe, intangible, it nevertheless has a great influence upon the picture. It is its soul, and hardly to be dealt with here. It is or it is not, as it so happens, except that we do know that some workers happen to get it time after time, while others do not. Sometimes the most prosaic individuals, men with meagre education, bring out picture after picture with this indescribable charm in them, and we are at a loss to understand just how they do it. They, themselves, do not know. It is a part of them which they are not at all acquainted with. It is as if they were for the time reincarnated in the spirit of some great artist, while they make their pictures, only to return to earth again when they are done; to their ordinary selves, plain, uninteresting, unable to make themselves clear with speech, yet they have an extraordinary lucidity of expression the minute they are with their pictures. They do not know composition, technique, and yet they make exquisite pictures, for all to be happy with. We get a faint understanding of what is meant by feeling when we mention that some musician lacks technical skill but gets richness of feeling. It is of the spirit rather than of the material self, ethereal, and not to be described by words. This is, of course, the greatest of qualities in a picture, the most powerful and desirable but, as said, it either is or is not, as it happens and nothing we can say will make it more or less. There is no question, however, that if we take some great artist in his incipient stage, we can, by training, make either an artist or a plumber out of him. He has both in his makeup. By teaching him a trade we make of him a master artisan, for he has something in him which, regardless of what he attempts, forces him to do all things well. We teach him to become an artist and his pictures are the kind that make men happy. They have in them a spirit which is different from others. They may be technically bad, and lacking in certain qualities of composition and thought, but they have the vital spark. By teaching this same man arrangement, composition, and sound technique we create genius. All great artists were beginners at one time; and made bad pictures.

So that vital spark, which we weakly call feeling, we must leave aside as beyond our control, except as we teach the worker technique and composition so that he may the more fully open up his heart to a world which is only too eager for real talent. Composition and technique are but the ink and words with which he may express himself.

We then turn to the thought of arrangement, or composition, having in a previous chapter touched upon technique. While these two branches are well wound up and tangled together, they must be considered separately, each as an item apart.

No matter what we do, we have to think of it before we do it, unless we decide to go aimlessly, as does the vagabond. There are vagabonds in art who make very good pictures. There are always those who choose to go happy-go-lucky without thought. The idea has certain advantages, especially that of spontaneity, and it never hampers the spirit or feeling of the action. It is, however, ill-considered to ramble along, trusting in an impotent providence for pictures. It is far surer to take some thought upon the matter, and has been proven a good thing. There is this conflict however, the free action of the spirit against the over-calculated action which fails for sheer lack of inspiration. There is the happy compromise, and there is also the idea that the worker by real effort and application can so assimilate the principles of composition that he uses them instinctively, forgetful of them, free to apply his entire feeling to the inspirational reactions in the picture. The last is the ideal case but very few have worked out their photography so that they can proceed carefree, vagabonds and yet not vagabonds, knowing that all is well with their pictures and that their dreams will work out easily upon the picture space. It is but a vision of the ideal, and we would hope to see the pictures of such a worker. So we solve many problems when the photographer learns his technique and composition so well that they become second nature with him and are forgotten, or as much.

No matter what we do, whether it should be the

LANDSCAPE
Fred R. Dapprich

GOTHIC
Author

making of a rug, the construction of a building or any other procedure, we must plan it, design it, so to speak. No matter what form that design takes, we call it composition when we speak of pictures. A bit of music is composed; a building must be designed, composed again; a rug must be designed or composed, and a business scheme must be planned or composed. Composition is everywhere in our daily life, and we cannot evade it. As mentioned, only the vagabonds can do that, and sometimes they succeed after a fashion, but those are exceptional cases. Everything must be worked out, composed.

But to think, to plan, to scheme too deliberately, is to become cold and calculating and to destroy the fibre of that part of us which desires pictures. Many of our well-known pictorialists are doing just this, and are making mechanical, rule of thumb pictures. It is because they have not learned their lessons well, and have come to accept certain formulæ for pictures which they know will work. We must learn to plan lightheartedly so that, when doing the work, we will not be under the stress of the knowledge that we are planning. We again approach the vagabond idea, so to speak, and we work out the picture, not realizing that we are doing it. It must not be a trouble. The real picture must be a work of happiness. There has been an unfortunate stress about it, a competition about it, which makes one worker try to exceed the other. It cannot be a contest and retain the art in it. We plan too viciously for our own good when we force, and are absorbed in the thought which we hoped would make the pictures. So when we plan we should not allow ourselves to become lost in planning, lest the very planning become the major thought. Pictures are the things we are after, pictures as made with the camera. It is a little new art which we are concerned with, and it must not become sordid. We do not even know that it will ever become recognized as an art, but we hope so, and we must be prepared to do the best we can with it, against the time when opportunity presents itself.

What is art? We do not know. We only know that when a man desires to do something which is an expression of his own, and that when he will make a great effort to do so, we call it art. It has been defined as "the expression of an emotional experience" whether justly or not. Art as we know it, is at least expression of what we do not know. Expression of something which is inside and which we do not understand, but which we must exude from ourselves, sometimes to the happiness and sometimes to the disgust of others. The camera worker feels the necessity of making a picture, and then he starts to think about doing it in such a manner that it will represent something which is entirely his. It is his expression. He does it, and it cannot be disputed that he does it in a manner which stamps the production as his own, unless he has copied. We can recognize the character of work of the better workers in photography. One makes his pictures with a certain stamp which is entirely his; another does pictures which tell us that he has made them.

190

FISHING BOATS—FULTON MARKET

Author

PORTRAIT—FRANK ROY FRAPRIE
Author

Most assuredly then, even such a mechanical instrument as the camera can be so handled as to make pictures which have an atmosphere about them, a quality which is individual. Perhaps some day they will hang in museums. We do not know, but we can make them so that they will stand as pictures. Then if the time ever comes when the great jury of common opinion says that photographs can be classed as pictures along with paintings, they will have been made so that they represent something worth while, and are equal to the award.

While the matter of composition seems, on the whole, to be merely applied geometry, as said by one great painter, and appears rather a mathematical matter, we are quite sure that we have a great control over the disposition of lines and masses. While they exist in the subject as unchangeable, apparently we can change them by modifying the perspective, by moving the viewpoint up or down, or sidewise. Nothing is fixed, even while it appears to be so. A straight line becomes a sloping line when we see it from an angle. It can even be a dot, or nearly so, as we choose to view it, or it can be a long, straight line as we select. A curved line is elliptical or a sharp angle as we would have it, the camera being movable. We are the designers of the lines and masses in the picture, no matter how fixed they are. They are as clay in our hands, the while immovable. Nothing is fixed in this world we live in.

So we can control all matters with this camera instrument, which takes only what it sees, realizing the fact that we are the masters of what it looks at, and can move it about here and there as we please.

Since it is a proven thing that the camera is not the precise instrument that the average person thinks, and that we can make a curved line into a straight line or a more severely curved line, or a straight line even into a dot, we logically come to the thought that we can begin to think about what kinds of lines, spots and masses will make a picture which will stand as a good one. That is composition.

The camera has as many virtues as faults, and while it is in a certain sense a rigid instrument, recording what it sees, it is evident that if we do succeed in arranging our items of subject matter into a real composition, it will take but a moment to record those items. We do not have to painstakingly draw the picture on canvas or paper. Whereas, the average artist has to create a picture and also set the boundary or frame around it so that they all relate properly, the camera has a frame already made to work to.

As we have said, a picture is a summary of items arranged to the creator's taste and set usually into a boundary or frame which must also compose with those items. The arrangement is simplified by the fact that the camera has the frame all made to set the composition into. Since nearly all items are movable, it simplifies matters a great deal if one of them is fixed and no trouble to compose. If the boundary, too, were a movable item we would have more difficulties, and nearly all the arts which deal with pictures have this item to worry about. Painting, drawing, etching, all have to set their own boundaries, and simple as this may seem, it is one of the most difficult portions of the work. The fact is, the average artist hardly thinks in terms of boundary until the picture is done, and is all engrossed in the general relation of items in his picture. The architect, for example, has a most vicious habit of drawing a picture first, and when it is all done, he sets a boundary around it in a most haphazard manner. Artists have done this for so long that they sometimes forget that the frame is part of the composition of their pictures.

So perforce we are to the point where we think about the fact that in photography we start with a frame and no picture, and that the object is to set into that frame a series of items, so arranged with respect to each other as well as to the frame, that the result will be compositional. We first consider the empty frame, the boundary with no picture in it, and there are many facts about it, so many that one could make a book of that subject alone.

Imprimis, the frame is usually rectangular, sometimes square but seldom, sometimes rectangular with rounded or arched top, but usually rectangular in shape, and of varying proportions. Men have been making pictures for many centuries, and have placed perhaps, ninety percent of them in rectangular frames. Whether the rectangular space is the best or not is of no consequence. There are many amateur philosophers who will argue that it is not necessarily

195

so. They will argue anything, and photography is rich in such characters. The fact is, that it does not matter whether it is actually so or not, except men have made it so by their thoughts. It is a curious thing that we like what we are generally fed with. Since the general harmony of any picture makes it palatable, and since we have been taught to accept the rectangular picture space as best, it is best, and any effort to change it would result in a dislike for the pictures. There must be some good reasons why this type of picture space is the best, although we cannot tell why right off. It is the best, and we like it the best.

Through the years that pictures have been made, much thought has been put into the consideration of the proportion of this rectangle and how each side should relate to the other. It was not done mathematically but by drawing out space after space through many years. After a long time it was found that these sides had a definite relation to each other and that if they were measured, a proportion which was more used than any other, could be established. This is exactly what happened.

Take, for instance, the oldest of the graphic arts, perhaps painting. That may throw some light upon this matter of proportion. Let us look at the stock sizes of canvasses, which one might buy in an art store. 12 x 16, 16 x 20, 18 x 24, 20 x 24, etc. That ought to tell us something. Taking the average proportion of these we see that they are nearly all of a certain proportion, about three to four, the first

EAST RIVER AND MANHATTAN BRIDGE

Author

PORTRAIT—NICKOLAS MURAY
Author

being exactly so, the second 3.2 to 4, the third 3 to 4, and the last 3.3 to 4. This leads us to the conclusion that the picture space has, after centuries of consideration, been reduced to a usable proportion, and that is about three to four. That this is the best general proportion we must admit as it is the consensus of opinion of many minds over a long period of years.

When the first camera was made, that is the first commercial camera, they were forced by the nature of the instrument to adopt some size of plate, and what was more natural than to turn to the older art for their information on the subject? We see that the sizes of cameras are very much the same in proportion as the canvasses of the painter. Taking the 2¼ x 3¼, the 3¼ x 4¼, the 4 x 5, the 5 x 7, and others, we see that they follow the idea of proportion as set by painters, being respectively 2.8 to 4, 3.05 to 4, 3.2 to 4, and 2.9 to 4. All the foregoing is to emphasize the fact that the photographic picture is one which is placed in a rectangular space and that the sides of that space have a certain proportion, which is more or less settled. Of all cameras the one which violates the above mathmatical thought is the postcard camera, the 3¼ x 5½, and it is very unpopular with pictorial workers, which more or less proves that the proportions set forth are right for the best work. The postcard camera fits in with no pictorial ideas, and was made not with any thought of real use, but merely as a selling proposition, to make a picture to fit the postcard.

So we reach the point where we accept the rectangular space as blank and that we are going to study the certain things which will fill it so that we get a picture. The size of camera is of no consequence, as we have established that all are more or less the same in shape, and one picture will do the same as the other except that the dimensions will be different.

We note that the space can be used vertically as well as horizontally, and that when we turn it either way it has an effect upon the picture. If we desire a landscape, nearly every time we will use a horizontal picture. When we desire a picture made within the narrow confines of the city street, we will use it vertically. Why? This deserves thought. We must take note of these curious facts. Of course, one side of the space is longer than the other. The fact that we make the picture horizontal seems to indicate that we describe the position of the picture by the way the long side lies. And when we make a vertical picture we stand the long side up, vertical. We again seem to describe the position of the picture by the position of the long side. It seems to be the important side. It is. The long side of the space is the controlling feature, and is the strong side. If we propose to take vertical lines in our picture, we naturally place the picture space so, and add to the feeling of verticality by using the long, strong lines of the space to accent and assist the vertical lines in the subject matter, to strengthen them, as it were. If we make a picture of a vertical object, and place it in a horizontal picture space, we lose altogether the feeling of the subject, since it has not been properly set down on the picture space. If we propose to make a picture of a marine subject, where the predominating lines in the subject are horizontal, we naturally follow the idea by placing the picture space also horizontal. On the other hand, if we try to make it vertical we lose the effect, and the vertical lines of the rectangle will fight against the horizontal lines of the subject. Thus the way we place the picture space has a great effect upon the result, and we see by this that the empty rectangle has a feeling of its own, not to be violated. The horizontal picture is restful, and the vertical more dramatic and restless.

Leaving all the foregoing aside, we will consider for ourselves this proportion of space and what its effect is, since we are working in a medium which, to all practical purposes, is new. Taking the supposed standard of 4 to 3, Fig. 1, we can note that it is of an

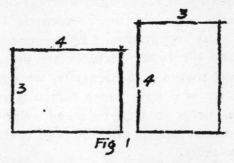

Fig 1

extremely rational and conservative shape, and that we would have no great difficulty in placing in either of these spaces a vertical or horizontal composition. The difference between the sides is not great and no intense accent is placed upon the fact that the picture space stands vertical when it is in that position or horizontal when it is so. It is moderate, not forced.

If we choose to draw a rectangle which has a more severe panel shape, Figure 2, we note immediately

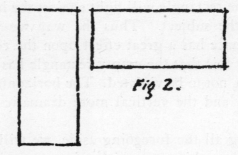

Fig 2.

that the accent is placed more forcibly upon the long lines. Strength is generally moderate. One of the greatest architects in the country is noted for the conservative quality of his design, whereas many struggling architects use the more eccentric forms and have far less reputation. Thus moderation is strength, and the better pictures are not placed in freaky panel shapes. Incidentally, we note that in this shape we will have more difficulty in placing the various items in well-balanced relation. The postcard camera has this trouble and is shunned by pictorial workers.

Having decided that the reasons for using a rectangular space are adequate, and that the space has

PORTRAIT—DR. RUZICKA
Author

EAST RIVER—MORNING
Author

been determined in a proportion which is reasonable, we may turn to the consideration of what we would put into the space. In the discussion it is best to use diagrams, realizing the weakness of words, or perhaps that most of us are eye-minded rather than ear-minded and understand diagrams better than descriptions.

We first take the horizontal space and think about what subjects we might place in it. Landscapes, marines, groups, sometimes still life, and sometimes even architectural subjects and portraits, but the last not so often. Always pictures where the horizontal lines predominate. Where the basic balance follows a horizontal direction we should follow it with the long side of the picture space, to strengthen the idea, and the same thought applies to the vertical line.

In some pictures we find a series of items which seem to have no relation to the edges of the picture, where the artist has perhaps made a drawing of some modishly decorative subject and, as an afterthought, has placed around it a line. Or perhaps, the publisher has put a line around it to make it conform with his magazine page. These are but decorative sketches, decorative as to subject matter only, and not as to general arrangement. They have not been completed with consideration of the frame, and are not compositions at all and should not be considered as such. We see many drawings on magazine pages, or covers, and they have no pictorial lesson that we can draw upon other than to establish the fact that certain forms are decorative and beautiful, and look

205

well to us. We file them away in our thoughts for future reference against the time when we can apply the idea to a study of the figure, or perhaps in the arrangement of a line in some landscape composition. For our part we must never forget the frame, or edge.

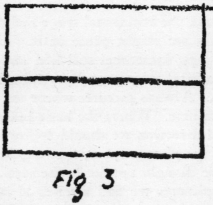

Fig 3

We then turn to the horizontal panel, Figure 3, and look into the effect of that most prominent thing in all picture work, the horizon line. While curiously enough, photography has a faculty of finding most of its compositional lines in the foreground, and the horizon is a matter which occurs in perhaps not over twenty percent of photographic pictures, it is a thing which must be studied and understood in order that the other matters in composition may be fully appreciated. Perhaps we draw the horizon line across the center of this panel and force ourselves to think about the line as so placed, its relation to the top and bottom sides, and what it does to the space between those lines. We have then taken the

THROUGH THE COLUMNS
Author

CHOPSTICKS
Author

most important step in photography, or any other
kind of picture making, toward the real thought
about balance and unity, and other matters. We are
forced to see that balance is at stake, and that this
line has a material effect upon the picture space.
It divides it in two, and we do not like it that way.
Something is the matter. We are tempted to remove
one of the portions and use that for the picture. It
feels bad. Balance and unity are being thought
about, and they are close friends. The thoughts
which are responsible for real pictures are with us,
even in this incipient stage. In spite of the fact that
the horizon line has been placed so that it cuts the
picture evenly in two and is a detriment to the
picture in that position, we note that it adds another
long horizontal line to the top and bottom sides, and
strengthens the feeling in the picture.

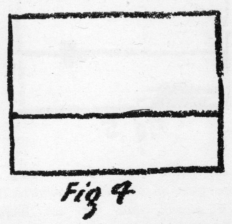

Fig 4

Now suppose we move the horizon line a little
lower in the space. Figure 4. We feel different

about it now. The picture is not divided in two parts and there seems to be some reason for the line being in that position. We have a feeling about it now, and the line seems alive and ready to do something good for the picture. It might even be a distant shore line. It now begins to do some work which adds to the picture. It has been placed with a certain thought or reason. Our sensibilities are affected more pictorially, so to speak. Where in the case of the evenly divided panel we had no impulse but to note that it was composed of two spaces of equal interest, neither of them strong enough to hold the attention, and further that it was merely a bit of paper with a line across it, we now seem to have a faint liking

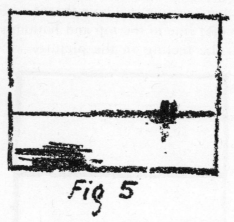

Fig 5

for the panel which is divided unevenly. It feels better. One portion has more interest than the other, more power, and we are happy with it. In order to make the discussion concrete, we will place two dots on the panel, as in

Figure 5, and show that even these are enough to create a pictorial thought. We have but a simple rectangle, one line across it which we call the horizon, and two spots placed upon it with a charcoal, yet it has a certain small, pictorial feeling. Why? Because they have been placed with a certain thought for what they will do as to balance and, while they mean nothing separately, together they begin to show that a picture is intended.

Suppose we now place the horizon line slightly above the center of the picture space, Figure 6.

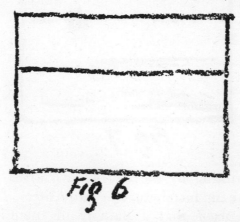

Fig 6

Again we see that in dividing the space unevenly we feel better about it. Interest is held. One portion is stronger than the other. We seem to be happiest when the line is any place but in the center. If we imagine for a moment that we are looking at a real picture, we see that the accent has been placed upon the foreground. Again let us make a few marks in the space and we see that we have created a feeling

of distance by accenting the foreground. So when
we consider the two cases, Figure 5, and Figure 7,
we note that the feeling of distance in a picture is
controllable by raising or lowering the position of
the horizon line. The principle is applicable to pictures of any subject, even to interiors of houses where
there would seem to be no horizon line. As it happens, the diagram Figure 7 is one of a very fine

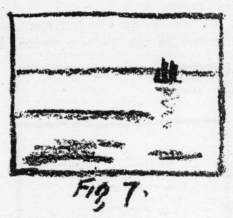

Fig 7.

marine painting by the well-known artist, and the
atmosphere in his picture is exquisite. This then
serves as proof that a paucity of material well-
handled will increase the atmosphere in a picture,
and that a complication of subject items tends to
decrease pictorial effect. The simple pictures are the
best by all means.

There are many pictures where the horizon line
does not appear at all, but one may rest assured that
it is there and that the feeling of it exists all the time,
if not in actual appearance, assuredly in impression.

THREE JUGS
Author

RAINY DAY—WASHINGTON SQUARE
Author

We cannot neglect it in any picture no matter what the subject.

Having made a brief survey of the horizon line when placed at or near the center, we can note the effect when it is moved to points nearer the top or bottom of the picture. Figure 8, and Figure 9. For the sake of simplicity and because one day the writer was impressed with a certain marine painting, let us suppose that we are concerned again with a marine subject. We see that in Figure 8 we have a picture

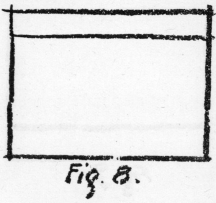

Fig. 8.

which is mainly foreground, and that we must use this position of the horizon mostly when there is important matter at that point which we desire to arrange into a picture, where the essential items are all near us. These are more eccentric forms of composition and are great favorites with many pictorialists. In Figure 9 we have accented the sky portion, perhaps for the reason that there is some essential feature there which we desire to have in our arrangement, a fine cloud, the bare space of the sky, which in many cases can be very powerful. If there is nothing there we would not have the horizon so low but would point the camera down, taking in the foreground. One of the reasons why so many pictorial workers have made foreground pictures is that there have been blank skies which they desired to avoid and they were forced to search for pictorial material elsewhere. Incidentally, photography is weak in handled the sky subject and it has been avoided as much as possible.

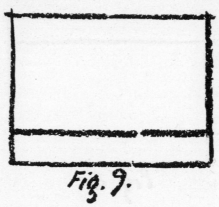

Fig. 9.

In examining Figure 8, as a pictorial possibility, we can by making a few marks see if it is feasible to use this position of horizon. The horizon is merely a dark line in any marine subject, and we show it as such. We now place a spot near it which might indicate a ship, and in the foreground a few more which might show a dock, with a figure or two and perhaps a boat tied to it. Figure 10. We have balance which is evident, a two-spot composition as it happens. The foreground is the interesting portion of the picture,

LANDSCAPE—A
Author

DISCUS THROWER
Author

is compatible with the position of the horizon, and the spot in the distance is used merely to assist in holding interest in the foreground items, to balance them into position as it happens. The spot of ship lures the gaze away for a moment, tempts it away, only to have it return again to the more important item in the foreground. Interest is accented in this manner and the picture does not become monotonous. The balance line between the two spots, while not evident, is there in effect and just as existent as if it were actually drawn.

Fig. 10.

Imagine for a moment, Figure 10, that the foreground spot is a tree. That the distant spot is another tree, and that a winding brook runs between the two, the horizon being in the same position. We have the same composition, except that the line between the two essential spots exists in this case.

Photography is especially strong in the foreground, as is almost any other method of making pictures, and to show this point more fully we have drawn the above diagrams so that the worker will take advantage of this easy way of making a picture. In this manner one can make many pictures in an afternoon's walk, with disregard for the weather or other conditions, when other pictures are unobtainable. The illustrations in the book do not seem to show this, and it is simply that the average worker has somewhat neglected this very charming composition.

Fig II

In order to avoid long, dry discourse on this subject, which would be so easy to fall into, we run along with occasional diagrams and in that way relieve the feeling of study. We could talk of balance, unity, mass, line and other items, but where it comes in casually in the general discussion of arrangement, the reader will remember it better and have the thoughts with him later on when he has his camera in hand. It is the purpose of this book to see if some few cannot do better pictures, practically, without making of it a long, tedious proceeding.

Suppose we draw another little space, disregarding the horizon as an item of importance. It can come any place, since it does not matter. Figure 11. We place in the space a figure, in the center laterally. It does not feel well there. It is not good. Many will tell us that this is so because it is in the center. The writer does not know this to be so, for he has seen many pictures with figures and other objects in the center and they were very good. The point is, that it does not feel right in this case. Suppose we move it to one side a little, Figure 12, and we

Fig 12.

like it much better. Why? Very few people know, and those who pretend to know usually do not. There are no rules, and what few thoughts we have on the subject are not laid down as rules. If the reader gets up a fine set of rules, he will be lost when he tries to make a picture, for he will find cases where no rule will cover. Better to have no rules, for pictures are not made that way.

The main thing is to get started thinking about the subject, and let us work out our own impressions and ideas, if there are to be any. Then they will be ours, of our own invention, to be used easily since we know them on account of having evolved them. Most persons have not thought of composition at all. If they did we would have more good photographs. All one has to do to make better pictures is to begin thinking about what makes a picture good or bad, and the rest is simple. The difficulty is to get people to think about a thing, and once that is done performance follows.

Fig 13.

In Figure 12 we moved the figure a little to one side to see if it made matters better. It did, but something was still lacking. Let us try adding another spot, another smaller figure to one side. Figure 13. It feels better that way, and is not so monoton-

HAMLET
Author

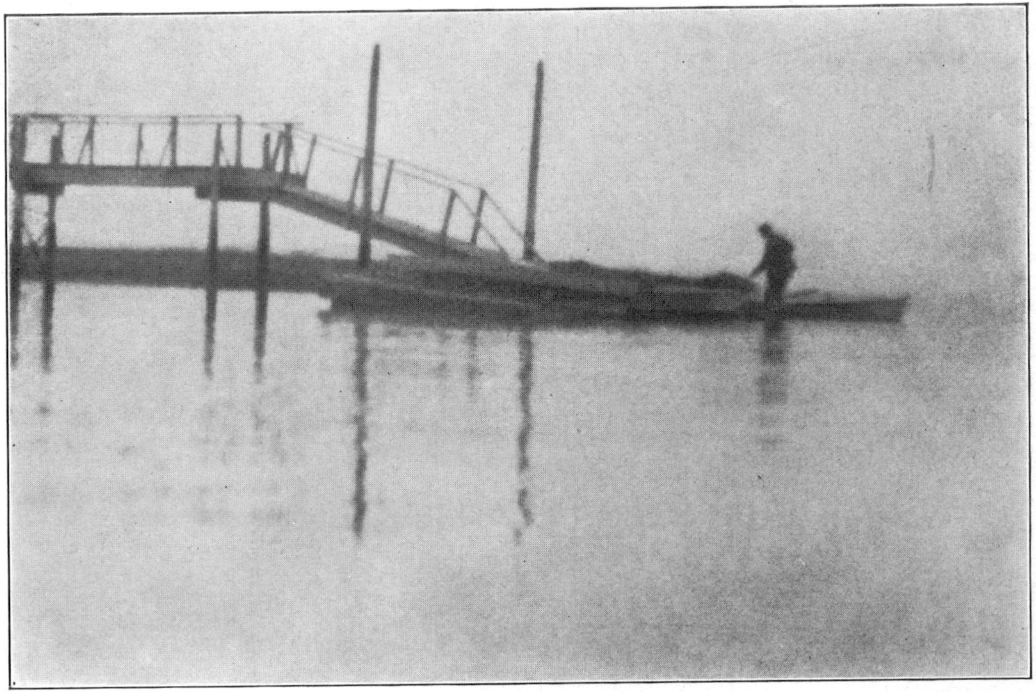

THE FISHERMAN

Author

THE END OF DAY
Author

FIRE FIGHTERS
Author

ous. We have the same conditions as in Figure 10, except that we are now on land. The one figure was bothersome, and one looked too intently at it. Another was a relief. The picture is not so fixed. For the same reason lights on the coast are made to flash intermittently, so that the eye will not be fatigued in looking at a fixed point too long. The fixed light disappears if one looks at it too long. The light does not go out, but the brain gets so tired trying to place the little light that the eye fails to record it. The lone figure is perfectly good composition, but it should be relieved, and the other figure does it. One must be of greater importance than the other, in order to hold the point of interest in one spot.

Fig 14.

Suppose we draw two figures in the picture, evenly spaced and of equal importance. Figure 14. It feels queer. One does not know where to look. Unity has been left out. There are two spots, and each one has as much power as the other.

227

The general study of composition is something which had better be made out at home, and if the worker will get a few bits of charcoal, and a pad of rough paper and spend an hour now and then making marks upon it, he will gain more than in many hours spent in the field with the camera. He can trace many things for line and spot composition. The study of shapes and their placing is important.

There was a great English artist who made a deep study of what he called the "line of beauty" and finally, after years of thought, he decided that it could all be summed up in one line, which was a reverse curve. That line represented beauty. Suppose we make a quick sketch, wherein we tell the same story, and it will be clearer. Figure 15.

Fig 15-

The reverse curve of the figure tells of what he called the line of beauty. We place it in the picture so, and relieve it with other marks so that it feels good, and is spaced well. The line of beauty alone is not enough, so it must be arranged into the picture.

The matter of composition is so varying, so difficult to describe, that it is really impossible. The few sketches are to get the reader trying to work out for himself what he thinks about it. His own thoughts are the best ones, for him, since they are his. All we can do is stir up matters and stimulate interest in the subject. Then, perhaps, we can create a desire to make pictures. The desire is the big thing. Lacking in all other matters it will carry the worker through. Perhaps a few of the pictures shown herein will intensify the desire to think about these things. In that case they will be more potent arguments than all the words we could write.

The chapter has been made brief, in the belief that the practical application is assuredly the thing which will influence the most workers. So we have been profuse in illustrations. Some of them are discussed so that we may further the study of practical composition and the general reasons for pictures.

CHAPTER VIII

DISCUSSION OF PICTURES

Realizing that most workers in photography are rather sensitive, the writer refrains from any discussion of their prints and has chosen to do so only with his own, since in that way he can express himself freely without hurting anybody's feelings. There is no print which is perfect, and the writer is a critical sort of person. If he said what he thought about the prints in the book he would wake up the morning after publication with no friends in photography.

So in discussing his own prints he can tear them to pieces with a critical pen, knowing only too well their deficiencies, and the reasons why they are so. The criticisms will therefore be the more illuminating since he can explain the reasons why there is this and that error. Many times pictures have to be taken with limitations accepted, or left entirely, and in these cases it will be interesting to note the reasons for failure.

1. *"Gothic."*

Illustrated on page 188.

An arched gothic entrance way in the Harkness Memorial Buildings at Yale University. Knowing

230

ENTRANCE—ST. THOMAS'
Author

IN A GARDEN
Author

the weakness of the average worker to know "where it was taken," we tell it in each case, not that it matters so much, as to satisfy the curiosity of the others. There is in this print no especial compositional arrangement, except that the feeling of the picture is such that it seems to carry the eye well enough. It was not taken for pictorial reasons but to reproduce the architecture of the buildings, a hundred pictures being taken on the trip. According to one authority a print has the best of reasons if it merely reproduces the subject.

2. *"Fishing Boats—Fulton Market."*

Illustrated on page 191.

The composition in this picture is rather too busy, but the feeling of the salt water and the boats is good. Rather a boast, but the writer has had some little experience with boats on salt water. The truth is there was not a complete choice of viewpoint, and this was the best that we could do with the subject. Otherwise it was to be left untaken, and it seemed too good for that. The feeling of line is not very plain, and certain deficiencies are visible, which were more or less unavoidable. The reflections seemed to be important, so the camera was deliberately pointed downward to get them, and also to avoid too much sky which would have destroyed balance. Cutting off the masts of the boat in this case is not objectionable.

3. *"Portrait—Frank Roy Fraprie."*

Illustrated on page 192.

This is a rather poor handling of the large head. Since it happens to be one of the luminaries of photography, the gentleman being the editor of a well-known photographic publication, it is the more unpardonable. The quality of the diffusion is good however, and the values are well held. It would seem that the head is a trifle low in the picture for real comfort. He insisted on being taken with his hat on, which complicated matters. There was no retouching in the picture.

4. *"East River and Manhattan Bridge."*

Illustrated on page 197.

The picture was taken with the motion picture camera on an October morning and then enlarged on bromide paper. There was no deliberate diffusion except to use a lens which would not cut sharp, and enlargement did the rest. A contact print would have appeared sharp. This is an instance where diffusion depends to a certain extent upon the degree of enlargement, and if a soft focus lens is used, stopped

PORTRAIT—MRS. Q.
Author

AN IMPRESSION OF BROOKLYN BRIDGE
Author

down so that it seems to work sharp, it will do this from the very small negative. Both negative and enlargement were made with the soft focus lens, used well stopped down. Compositionally the picture feels good, and the values are forced a little in development to obtain the feeling of misty distance.

5. "Portrait—Nickolas Muray."

Illustrated on page 198.

There is nothing unusual in the composition of this portrait, except that it is a brutal likeness of the man, and shows him as he is. He admits it, which proves nothing. The outstanding feature of the picture is the proper use of the much-abused soft focus lens, the picture being made at f 4.5. No retouching was done. The tone of the whites in the shirt front is too bright, and could be reduced a little to avoid drawing attention from the face, which should be the important item. The spacing of the picture seems to be good.

6. "Portrait—Dr. Ruzicka."

Illustrated on page 203.

There is nothing special to say about this in any respect. It is neither good or bad. The values are well held, and there is good detail in all portions of the print. Dr. Ruzicka sat down for three minutes one day, and but two plates are exposed, this being one of them. The lens quality is good, there being no halo, a thing to be avoided under all circumstances. The picture was taken at f 4.5 with an adjustable lens, adjusted for full diffusion.

7. *"East River—Morning."*

Illustrated on page 204.

This was taken with the motion picture camera, and a direct enlargement made from one of the frames. It is effectively, but rather crudely composed, dramatic rather than anything else, which makes up for many deficiencies in the eyes of the unsophisticated. No great attempt was made at a refinement of arrangement and the camera was set up quickly and turning started as the derrick was being pulled out of the picture. Sometimes one must work quickly, or lose it altogether. If there is any composition, it is the repetition of vertical lines through which we seem the dim outlines of the bridge.

8. *"Through the Columns."*

Illustrated on page 207.

This photograph of the Woolworth Tower from the peristyle of the Municipal Building, is simply an architectural subject, using the two buildings together to accomplish a composition which is rather more dramatic than good. The writer has the peculiarity, that he will at any time forsake good arrangement to get dramatic effect, which shows in all his work. While this is not a terrible sin, it is not too good, and it is not recommended to the worker. Curiously enough it makes pictures which are very acceptable to the lay mind and, where they would cast aside better composed and thought out pictures, they will accept these. However, good composition and idea is by far the better way and pictures result from it which will live longer.

Each worker has his own way of doing and the writer has had a curious training in making pictures which were for immediate effect, having done much magazine work, where the life of the picture was not of so much moment as its ability to punch hard for a short time. Contrasts well handled will do it.

9. "Chopsticks."

Illustrated on page 208.

A brass bowl, some chopsticks and a ten cent fan are the materials used in this picture. Again we have, not so much a good composition, as a queer arrangement which is effective. Queer shapes seem to be one formula for successful photographs, and as such will pass any "jury salon, they being very susceptible to the unusual." Not knowing how to place it they pass it through. Juries are queer things after all, and you can take six intelligent persons and put them together and out of it, instead of getting the intelligence of all six, you do not get as much as has any one of them. It is the curious failure of many minds together. This picture has no basic balance and is but a curious set of lines which are difficult to judge. It really is not a picture at all, but has received favorable comment.

10. *"Three Jugs."*

Illustrated on page 213.

Nothing much can be said of this picture, except that it is technically good, which is something after all. It is a sort of three-spot composition which usually succeeds, if the spots are placed at all well. The main thing about it is that the simple subject has been saved from the scrap basket by control of values. The exposure was medium full, but not too much so, and development carried just far enough to make sufficient negative to print; just so thin that printing became a task as it were. This is one way to make the best of any subject, and a method of Dr. Ruzicka.

11. *"Rainy Day—Washington Square."*

Illustrated on page 214.

First of all it has a bad title. There is no reason to mention where it was taken and the effect upon

SCENE FROM HAMLET
Author

SOUTH STREET—NEW YORK
Author

others is bad. It might be any place and so the title is foolish. It is merely a study in balance, and not too good, except that people seem to like it.

12. *"Landscape"—Marked A*

Illustrated on page 217.

No special composition, except the use of the familiar artifice of using a white spot upon a dark ground. It is a thing one does when nothing better can be thought of. Made years ago and it is a fine example of immature picture making. The tree on the left is stiff and of bad shape, but in those days the writer was only too tickled to find something which came near being a picture.

13. *"Discus Thrower."*

Illustrated on page 218.

The reason for this picture is peculiar. Mrs. Harry Payne Whitney, in whose studio garden this was taken, sent all her statues off to Newport for an exhibition, and the one which ordinarily stood upon the pedestal was gone. The writer was making some photographs there and what was more natural than to replace the statue with a living model? The model happened to be the dancing partner of Pavlowa, and

243

he knew more about this kind of photography than the writer. This is the picture and perhaps the most interesting thing about it is the way it happened to be made. It has no compositional value, and is again the familiar white spot on a dark ground.

14. *"Hamlet."*

Illustrated on page 223.

Walter Hampden as Hamlet. The picture was made on the stage with normal lighting as used in the play. On a hypersensitized plate the exposure was about one-half second at f 6. The figure was the thing to be dealt with, and enough of the set was included to see if the atmosphere of the character could not be held. The dark space at the top seems to do more work than any other portion of the picture except the figure, which, of course, is all important. In fact, the picture was made by Mr. Hampden rather than by the writer.

15. *"The Fisherman."*

Illustrated on page 224.

Simple composition, rather weak as to balance, but holding the atmosphere of the salt water, which carries it.

AN ENTRANCE
Author

ENTRANCE—TEMPLE OF THE SCOTTISH RITE
Author

16. "The End of Day."

Illustrated on page 225.

Salt water again, holding the feeling, and better in compositional values than some of the others. Simple two-spot arrangement, with horizontal lines of the sandy shores to assist. The picture was made with the motion picture camera, and one of the frames enlarged directly on bromide paper, from which this reproduction was made. It was schemed, and to hold the feeling of the sea, the figure dressed in "oilers," was introduced in spite of the fact that it was a dry, sunny day.

17. "Firefighters."

Illustrated on page 226.

Another picture made from a frame of film taken with the motion picture camera. The writer was going to the country and happened to bump into a fire, and made some film of it for pictorial effect. This is another case of where dramatic, rather than compositional values hold the picture up, but it is effective.

18. "Entrance, St. Thomas'."

Illustrated on page 231.

Architectural pure and simple, taken for no reason except that the writer was attracted by it as he is by all architectural subjects. The Gothic is perfect, or nearly so, and there was little to do except to get a lighting which would hold it together. The figures in the foreground are placed to give scale, and indicate size.

19. *"In a Garden."*

Illustrated on page 232.

White spot against dark ground. Other than that there is nothing to say that this is a good picture. The lens quality is very bad, being of a poor quality of diffusion. This is a case where the soft focus lens was abused, but the halftone may not show it.

20. *"Portrait—Mrs. Q."*

Illustrated on page 235.

Simple portrait, simple lighting, without retouching or any attempt made to change values. It is nothing unusual except that the entire effect was accomplished by using a black background. Note that in all cases dark grounds have been used for portraits. Nothing should be used to detract from the person.

21. *"An Impression of Brooklyn Bridge."*

Illustrated on page 236.

Taken with the motion picture camera using a soft focus lens, and then enlarged again using a soft focus lens to about 6 x 8, from which this cut was made. Example of extreme diffusion, eliminating all detail, and holding just the main masses. Three tones in the picture, which is what was sought after. The feeling of distance accomplished by this method is apparent.

22. *"An Entrance."*

Illustrated on page 245.

Technically right, values good, figure well placed and posed, and compositionally not bad. But it is as bad as it is possible to make a picture, for the figure is Greek of the period 700 B. C. while the setting is Italian Renaissance of about 1500 A. D. for which there is no forgiveness. The writer slipped a cog when he made this picture.

23. *"South Street—New York."*

Illustrated on page 242.

Study of figures in a rough surrounding. Feeling of composition is that of two spots, and the picture has a curious set of lines which contradict each other here and there. Nevertheless it feels good, and passes muster for that reason.

24. *"Scene from Hamlet."*

Illustrated on page 245.

Again the picture is mostly made by the actors. Taken under natural stage lighting with hypersensitized plates and an exposure of about one-half second at f 6. Placing of figures in regard to the set was the only thing done by the writer. Keeping the figures low in the picture helped the dramatic value.

25. *"Entrance—Temple of the Scottish Rite."*

Illustrated on page 246.

Compositionally fair only, with lack of balance. There should be a dark note in lower right hand corner to hold the picture together. An architectural subject where the feeling, which is especially fine, was accomplished by the designer of the building. Odd subject, as it happens, and holds up for that reason, since it fails as a composition.

26. *"Still Life."*

Illustrated on page 251.

"Nothing unusual in this picture in any way, arrangement or otherwise. Technically it is not so

STILL LIFE
Author

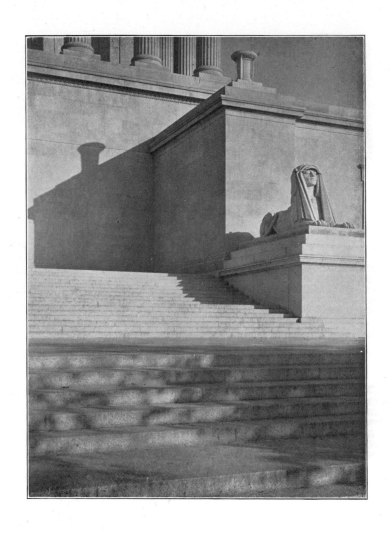

SPHINX—TEMPLE OF THE SCOTTISH RITE
Author

bad, and perhaps that is its best reason for existence. It must not be forgotten that good technique often justifies a picture."

27. *"Sphinx," Temple of the Scottish Rite.*

Illustrated on page 252.

This is nothing but an architectural subject so placed as to present an unusual set of lines and masses. The subject is unusual, which is a great deal to the picture. This is sharp. It could as well be soft, but I chose to make it sharp assuming that the detail is important. Architecture is always theatrical, and dramatic. In fact, it has been called the most theatrical of all the arts.